Dedicated, as always, to my family
my books would ne'

C000299732

Norman A Journey Through Time

Alex Askaroff

Norman A Journey Through Time

Alex Askaroff

Copyright © 2011 Alex Askaroff

First published in Great Britain in 2011

Churchill and D-Day photographs with kind permission from the Churchill Archive, Station X, Bletchley. Utah and war pictures courtesy of the Imperial War Museum.
Personal photos courtesy of H N Albone.

For more information on Alex Askaroff visit Sewalot.com, Amazon or Google.

Other early titles by the author

Random Threads Volume I Patches of Heaven
ISBN 0-9539410-4-3

Random Threads Volume II Skylark Country
ISBN 0-9539410-2-7

Random Threads Volume III High Streets & Hedgerows
ISBN 0-9539410-3-5

Tales from the Coast UK
ISBN: 978-0-9539410-5-6

Corner of the Kingdom
ISBN: 978-1-61179-067-2

Sussex Born and Bred
ISBN: 978-1-935585-22-0

Books published containing the author's work

A Celebration of Childhood Rivacre Paperback
Natural Peace Anchor Books Paperback
Poetry of Kent Millfield Paperback
This Natural World Arrival Press Hardback
South East Poets Arrival Press Hardback
Let's do Lunch Remus new fiction Paperback
Anchor Poets Anchor Books Hardback
This Vanishing World Poetry Now Hardback
Web of Thoughts Anchor Books Hardback
The Good Ol' Days Arrival Press Hardback
New Rhymes for Arrival Press Hardback
A Tapestry of Thoughts Spotlight Paperback
Mixed Musings Poetry Now Hardback
Special Occasions Arrival Press Hardback

The Original Random Threads Trilogy, packed full of Alex's stories

1. PATCHES OF HEAVEN ISBN 0-9539410-4-3

2. SKYLARK COUNTRY ISBN 0-9539410-2-7

3. HIGH STREETS & HEDGEROWS ISBN 0-9539410-3-5

To See Alex Askaroff's latest titles search Amazon and Google

Foreword

It has always fascinated me how strange and tangled our lives are. I have known Norman, who this story is about, for many years. He lives in Church Street just up the road from me. For the first few years we just nodded to each other when passing. Eventually we threw in "Good Morning." Then, "How are you today?" After what seemed like years we would stop and chat. During our chats we found common threads in our lives.

Both his sons had gone to my old school. My favourite teacher there, Rex Lord, was a friend of his. Norman had also been a teacher and had taught one of my brothers at Ratton School. Slowly other threads appeared as we talked, like the love of playing squash in our youth, boxing and one abiding joy that we both had—cycling.

As the years shot by in that annoying but unstoppable way, I learnt more about the small quiet man who now lives alone along the road, and a short 26 years later I had gained a huge amount of knowledge about my neighbour.

The Official Secrets Act had kept many an old fighter quiet. Their lips sealed, sworn to secrecy on royal orders, but with the passing of time and easing of laws those secret days sometimes come to life.

It has been a great privilege to be taken into Norman's confidence and to join him on his journey, to relive those special moments that make up our limited number of days on planet earth. Some journeys are in the mind and some with the body, his ability to remember events and dates is astounding and we must forgive any inaccuracies in a lifetime's worth of amazing detail. There is no doubt that had he written down events that occurred during his war years at the time and not 70 years later, they would have been in even more detail.

Like many people who live amongst us Norman had lived a life which he thought of as ordinary. He, like many of us, is almost invisible, a single leaf on a tree in our human forest. For most of the 20th Century Norman had been involved in and witnessed a brave new world, a world in which we live today.

Here is a mini biography of a modest man who was born into a rural time hardly changed for centuries. Where a team of farmers and animals would spend back-breaking days working a field, to a time when one man in an air-conditioned cosy tractor, with music playing on his iPod, guided by satellites in space, could do the same work in a few hours. Norman's journey has spanned the most interesting century that this planet may ever have, and provides us with a unique portrait of one man's life.

During Norman's trip through life I often digress to bring you events and topics that had such an influence on our world. Come with me on a journey through time.

Chapter 1
The Early Years

Norman was born in the picturesque and bustling market town of St Neots, Cambridgeshire, on Nov 28, 1919. The town, centred round the impressive market square, was lit by gas lamps and studded with churches. Dozens of pubs watered the thirsty farmers on market day. It was an idyllic place for a child to grow. He was a '*demob*' or '*celebration*' baby after his dad arrived back from serving as a photographer in the Royal Flying Corps during the First World War. Countless happy servicemen returning to their wives produced the first baby boom in Britain. He was christened Harold Norman Albone after his Uncle Harold.

Albone is an old Bedfordshire name and both his mum and dad had been born in Biggleswade. Norman never bonded with his first christian name and, much to his Mum's annoyance, used Norman so often that she gave up trying to change it back. It did not last however as at school he was nicknamed '*Ernie*' after his Dad. Dealing with his Mum was no problem but having a whole school call you Ernie was a situation impossible to change, so, for a while anyway, Norman just put up with it.

Norman is one of the last of the Victorians. His parents were Victorian as were most married couples having children during that period. Norman was really attached to a part of the old Empire that today seems like a million years ago, but in reality is just a simple step across the ages. As Norman talked to me about his parents I felt as if I knew them, and yet they had been brought up in a world where electricity had yet to triumph and the loo was a bucket at the bottom of the garden.

Norman nearly never made it to school, as the dreadful influenza pandemic was killing millions just after the war. In Britain nearly 250,000 people died of the dreaded Spanish Flu. Although it was a worldwide pandemic, it was called Spanish Flu after the King of Spain caught it. No one is sure how many millions died, but many more died from Spanish Flu than died during the World War that had just come to an end.

When Norman was just a snippet of a lad, the Great Ouse which snakes its way through the flatlands of Cambridgeshire towards St Neots decided to flood. He was rescued in the nick of time from an upstairs room. He was lifted out of the window into a punt as loaves of bread and half full bottles and pans floated around him.

Later, aged five, he had a brush with the old river again. He fell into the Ouse while horsing around with friends. A tree had fallen, partially across the river, and made a tempting bridge. Norman slipped and was going down to his watery grave. As he slowly sunk he watched the green water slowly darken to black. Suddenly the water lightened again and he was moving upward toward the light. He was dragged to safety by a passing walker who muttered a few words and, soaked, walked on. Unknown to Norman this close proximity to water was to have a huge impact on his later life.

"It's a funny old business—life." Norman once told me and how right he is. Norman was born lucky or charmed and through the years, time and time again it played a major part in his life. Norman was blessed with a special gift that Emperor Napoleon always sought out when picking his generals.

On his birthday Norman and his parents would gather around the radio to hear the announcer read out a list of people who had birthdays on that day. Radio was new in the mid 1920's and just a small concern so you could, for a shilling, write in and have your child's birthday announced. Norman would be glued to the set and eventually the announcer would say something like, "And young Norman Albone in St Neots is seven today. Norman your present is hidden in the camera box in the studio. Happy birthday."

He would then excitedly rush off to where his dad had hidden his present.

Years later it made sense why his father would always take the accumulator up the High Street to be recharged before his birthday; it was so the wireless would work perfectly with a fully charged battery.

The Studio in St Neots High Street was also the place they lived above. Ernest earned a meagre living taking wedding photos and portraits. When he first started his shop he only had a bicycle, so he would cycle to weddings with his reflex cameras and tripods balanced and tied around his bike. On more than one occasion strange looks followed him as he arrived at the church.

In the 1920's Ernest carried all his equipment on his bicycle to weddings.

Next to the shop was his Studio for those all important photos of families and local dignitaries. Ernest kept a glove-puppet handy for the kids and would mesmerise them with one hand working the puppet, while the other deftly opened and closed the lens cover. If a flash was needed, then he would carefully fill a pan with magnesium powder that was triggered by a battery which made the room light up with a whoosh, and smell like some old wizard's workshop.

At the back of the shop was the dark room where he would spend hours developing his pictures in a laboratory full of chemicals.

After developing his pictures he would take them to his framing area and make the frames and cut the glass for them.

Independent and practical, Ernest's shop was just one of the many small specialist shops that filled St Neots High Street in the 1920's. Norman knew them all in his high street playground. They were all important men in their day and many families in St Neots will be descended from them. There was Willy the grocer, Wise the chemist. Two butchers, Eays, who displayed turkeys plucked to the neck at Christmas and pigeon, pheasant, rabbit and hare the rest of the year and Neavson the pork butcher. Then there was Hamilton the furniture man, Wren the smelly fishmonger, Plumb's café where a cuppa cost a penny, which led along to the Picture Palace and the Market Square where the cattle market was held every week.

At the Picture Palace a violinist and pianist would accompany the silent films and play light music during the intervals when ice cream was served up and down the isle. There was the sweet & "baccy" shop, Fairweather's with a fine selection of pipes displayed in the window. Harrison, Cross & Veitch doctors, Sharp & Griffin the dentists. The *"gas chamber"* was always to be avoided if possible. Both the doctor's surgery and the dentists did more work on market day than the rest of the week combined as farmers from the outlying areas descended on the town. In the early part of the 20th Century people still saved for children's 21st birthdays to have all their teeth pulled and false teeth fitted. Can you imagine what a present that was!

Ibbett was the local greengrocer who supplied fresh produce in season. A tomato at Christmas was impossible in the 1920's. Lynn was the powerful ironmonger who made whatever you wanted from a horseshoe to a steel ring to put through a bulls nose.

All legal proceedings, whether buying a horse or selling of land was handled by Wade, Gery & Brakenbury the local solicitors. They would cut up their indentures or contracts between the parties by hand giving each person entitled a piece of the contract. Each piece had a unique cut and so when the paperwork came back as a whole the cut documents came together like a puzzle. Simple but effective.

Finally the smartest building in St Neots was the Cross Keys Hotel, which ran a regular coach service to the railway station to pick up and drop off guests.

Ernie Wise, one of two High Street chemist shops had a sign in his window that read...

Here I lie with my two daughters,
Died through drinking Cheltenham waters.
Had I stuck to Epsom Salts,
We wouldn't be beneath these vaults.

One market day Mr. Wise popped out of his shop and left the young boy in charge. This was not unusual as he would often deliver customers pills. Suddenly a large farmer burst into the shop clutching his belly. "I need some salts boy where is Wise?"

"He has just pooped out sir. He will be back presently."

"Presently! I need relief now where is the Epsom Salts."

"I am sorry sir I am not allowed to prescribe drugs."

"Idiot. Hand me an ounce of the salts and be fast about it."

The young lad in a state of trepidation measured out the ounce of Epsom Salts and handed it to the country gentleman who rushed out and over the road to the pub. Sometime later Ernie Wise returned and the young lad explained the encounter to him. "My God boy, an ounce will go straight through him I'll have to track him down and let him know. Which way did he go?"

"No need sir. He went straight into the pub drank the salts and has been gripping the lamppost opposite ever since. I think he's too scared to move." The young lad pointed to the farmer on the opposite side of the road and they both burst out laughing.

To make ends meet at the photographic shop and to supplement the shop's mortgage payments, besides the usual photo frames and pictures, Norman's parents also sold china and kitchenware. Hilda would also do the washing in an old copper heated on the stove then use the scrubber and mangle before ironing with irons heated by the fire. It was non-stop work.

Ernest's shop opened six days a week and rarely closed before eight each night. They were long hours and little money but they survived and eventually with help from George Page, the assistant, cycling trips to the weddings became a little more balanced.

Norman and his Dad at Skegness in 1925. Within a few years
Norman would be back here training for war.

When Norman was nearly ten his dad took him up to the steeple
of the church near to his shop. They made their way up the winding
stairs, passed the bells, to the very top of the parapet. They surveyed
the wide open areas and outlying fields from their crows nest. "See
over there Norman." His dad said pointing, far away into the
distance towards a large castle. That's Kimbolton and that's where
you will go to school."

Chapter 2 Boarding School

Norman's first day at his new school also coincided with a momentous event in the young boy's life. He had his first trip in a motor car, something of a novelty as cars were rare in St Neots in 1929. He had seen the odd machine come and go and had run down the street chasing the modern marvel of our time, but had never been in one. It was his trip to boarding school but he was so fascinated by the speed of the car as it drove the seven miles to Kimbolton and the amazing sights that sped by that he had little time to worry.

From September 1929 until July 1936 Norman boarded at the ancient Kimbolton School, which has a proud history dating back to 1530, though not comprehensively recorded until 1600.

Nearby was where Catherine of Aragon spent her last years away from her philandering husband, King Henry. Right up until her early death she fought with Henry to keep her position by his side as the rightful Queen of England. Why anyone would want to be near a man responsible for the murder of thousands is most strange. The charismatic King obviously had two very different sides to him. No one would ever want to be on his bad side as it meant a one way trip to the executioner!

Kimbolton School has taught all classes of people, from dukes to air vice marshals, farmers to successful inventors. The school bred and still breeds that British kind of pupil who goes on to help run the empire. In the playground the kids would sing *"When good Queen Bess was on the throne Kimbolton was already brick and bone."*

Norman moved into the long dormitory for his first night with the other boarders. His housemaster, H E Day kept a close eye on him as he settled in. The toilets were buckets and the dining hall was often split in two and used by matron. Norman found that the school was spread out all over the little village with buildings everywhere like Mandeville House, White House or Corner House. Each morning he would set off with his school books to whichever building, like Cyril Gibbard for maths. Only later did the school take over Kimbolton Castle.

Norman's headmaster was the fearsome and mildly eccentric William Ingram. Ingram was the headmaster from 1913 until 1947.

He was admired and feared by the pupils in equal amounts. Norman always remembered him as a willowy formidable man who ruled with gentle strength. If William Ingram entered a room—silence was immediate! Ingram, a passionate headmaster, had a lot of contacts which he called upon when needed.

Ingram was always calling on the services of the local photographer who just happened to be Norman's dad. Ernest had apprenticed in Evesham before moving to his own shop in St Neots. A deal was eventually struck between the headmaster and the photographer. The photographer's son got into Kimbolton almost free, and the headmaster got all his school photos—almost free.

The deal between Norman's father and the school proved to have a huge effect on the whole of Norman's life. Also years later, inspired by his Dad, he took his own camera with him on his journeys. The pictures he took add thousands of words to his story.

Sports day at Kimbolton School. One of the many pictures that Ernest took for the school. The redoubtable William Ingram on the left next to the imposing figure of local farmer and chairman of the governors, William Whitehead.

Sports stars of the time were brought in to train the pupils. Tom "*Dancer'* Parker the Arsenal captain for football, the Welsh Flyweight boxing champion Jimmy Wilde known as "*The Mighty Atom'* and Jack "*The Master'* Hobbs, the England cricketer who is still considered the greatest opening batsman of all time. They all came to Kimbolton to train the pupils. Norman excelled at school and as the years raced by he won medals in boxing and football.

Kimbolton Senior School is now based in the grounds of Kimbolton Castle, and the preparatory school is at the other end of the village, connected via a beautiful tree-lined pathway known as The Duchess Walk. The School motto is *Spes Durat Avorum* (the hope of our ancestors endures).

Ingram cared deeply about his pupil's future and made huge efforts to find jobs for the leaving young men. His connections in London with the Zurich Insurance Company saw several school leavers obtain jobs there.

All too soon Norman's school years were over and he would be one of the boys found a job in London.

Chapter 3 A working life

In 1936, after King George V had died and amid rumours that his son, the new King Edward VIII, was having a relationship with an American woman, Norman left home and headed for the smoke filled streets of London.

Later in the year the nation, and world, shuddered when news reached them that the King was intending to run away with the divorcee, Wallis Simpson.

King Edward's December abdication shook the Empire. Prime Minister, Stanley Baldwin, had made it clear to Edward that it would be impossible for him to remain King if he decided to marry a twice-divorced American of uncertain character. Stanley Baldwin had never liked Edward and never warmed to the young man. His rebellious ways were not in tune with Baldwin's Victorian ideals of how a monarch should behave.

Edward was head-over-heels in love and made the decision to marry the girl of his dreams. He summoned Baldwin to Buckingham Palace. The Prime Minister rushed there in his big black overcoat and beaver skin top hat to hear Edwards's terms to stay as King. When they were rejected Edward made the decision that would stun the world.

His abdication announcement reverberated around our planet on wirelesses and in every printed newspaper from Australia to Iceland. The astounding speech was printed over and over again to a disbelieving world. He was the first British king since the time of the Anglo Saxons to voluntarily abdicate.

The speech that shook an empire.

Edward VIII - December 11, 1936

"At long last I am able to say a few words of my own. I have never wanted to withhold anything, but until now it has not been constitutionally possible for me to speak.

A few hours ago I discharged my last duty as King and Emperor, and now that I have been succeeded by my brother, the Duke of York, my first words must be to declare my allegiance to him. This I do with all my heart.

You all know the reasons which have impelled me to renounce the throne. But I want you to understand that in making up my mind I did not forget the country or the empire, which, as Prince of Wales and lately as King, I have for twenty-five years tried to serve.

But you must believe me when I tell you that I have found it impossible to carry the heavy burden of responsibility and to discharge my duties as King as I would wish to do without the help and support of the woman I love.

And I want you to know that the decision I have made has been mine and mine alone. This was a thing I had to judge entirely for myself. The other person most nearly concerned has tried up to the last to persuade me to take a different course.

I have made this, the most serious decision of my life, only upon the single thought of what would, in the end, be best for all.

This decision has been made less difficult to me by the sure knowledge that my brother, with his long training in the public affairs of this country and with his fine qualities, will be able to take my place forthwith without interruption or injury to the life and progress of the empire. And he has one matchless blessing, enjoyed by so many of you, and not bestowed on me — a happy home with his wife and children.

During these hard days I have been comforted by her majesty my mother and by my family. The ministers of the crown, and in particular, Mr. Baldwin, the Prime Minister, have always treated me with full consideration. There has never been any constitutional difference between me and them, and between me and Parliament. Bred in the constitutional tradition by my father, I should never have allowed any such issue to arise.

Ever since I was Prince of Wales, and later on when I occupied the throne, I have been treated with the greatest kindness by all classes of the people wherever I have lived or journeyed throughout the empire. For that I am very grateful.

I now quit altogether public affairs and I lay down my burden. It may be some time before I return to my native land, but I shall always follow the fortunes of the British race and empire with profound interest, and if at any time in the future I can be found of service to his majesty in a private station, I shall not fail.

And now, we all have a new King. I wish him and you, his people, happiness and prosperity with all my heart. God bless you all! God save the King!"

His younger brother, who was to become George VI, was also Edward's closest confident. He reluctantly became the third monarch from the House of Windsor, King and Emperor. He bestowed the title of Duke of Windsor on his brother.

There was another blow for the new King. His abdicating brother, the boy who had shared so many hardships with him, so many painful years of youth, his closest friend while he was growing up, the man who was the first to lend an ear when needed, packed his bags and ran from England. A warship took him to his lover in France and he married Wallis on 3 June 1937. They stayed together until death.

The Duke and Duchess of York at Brooklands racing circuit shortly before the abdication.

Norman's world had also changed from the quiet almost rural life of St Neots and Kimbolton to the mad rush of one of the world's great capitals, London. The very air was electric with nightclubs, jazz bars, casinos and pubs. London was alive with noise, action and controversy.

Oswald Mosley and his notorious Blackshirts were marching through the East End causing havoc, but Londoners stood shoulder to shoulder to block him and his fascists supporters. All manner of people locked arms together, bearded Orthodox Jews clasped the huge arms of rough Irish Dockers, and Catholics held hands with Protestants, men and women of all creeds and races rallied to stop the march. *They shall not pass*," was the cry that filled the heated air. It became known as the Battle of Cable Street and many from both sides ended up in prison. The Public Order Act was later passed to stop military uniforms being used in marches like Mosley's.

Mosley was later arrested and spent most of the war in a house in the grounds of Holloway Prison with his beautiful wife the

Honourable Lady Mosley, Diana Mitford. They had been married in 1936 at the home of Joseph Goebbels with Adolf Hitler as guest of honour. Diana Mitford was one of the six, often scandalous, Mitford Sisters.

Till her dying day Diana Mitford never renounced her belief in fascism.

It was a huge wrench at 16 to leave home and go to the big city, but Norman's life had been planned, and lodgings had been arranged at a hostel in South London. Norman worked all week for one pound and five shillings at Zurich Insurance. His lodgings were cramped with four-to-a-room but on the up side the cost of a-pound-a-week rent also included breakfast and an evening meal to boot.

The cost of Norman's lodgings left him with little to live on. When time and money allowed he would rush off to the cinema to see the latest Errol Flynn or Douglas Fairbanks film. But eating out, even in 1936, unless it was tea and chips, was kept for special occasions.

Singing in the Kazani Club at the time was a pretty young girl called Vera Lynn. Her elocution-perfect voice would drift out into the London night air and was sometimes broadcast over the radio. After the nightclub closed each night she would jump on the bus back to East Ham where she lived with her mum and dad. Before long Vera Lynn would be outselling the greatest stars of the age like Bing Crosby. During the war that was just around the corner, grown men would cry when they heard her sing with her pure voice which tugged straight at the heart strings. She symbolised the girl next door to a nation with her nostalgic songs. She would later become the *forces' sweetheart*.

Vera Lynn became the forces sweetheart with her patriotic and heart-tugging songs.

Chapter 4

Norman's starting wage was £60 a year with most of it going on lodgings, so he needed a cheap form of transport. One of his older school colleagues who had also found work with Zurich two years earlier, Dixon P Morris, had a superb Hetchins bicycle he no longer needed as, along with his brother J A V Morris, they were buying an Ariel Red Hunter motorcycle. Norman started saving every penny he could. Lunch was milk and a bun and after work straight back to his digs to save for the bicycle.

One night, one of the lads rushed into the digs in Sydenham. "Quick, quick, Crystal Palace has gone up like a tinder box." Norman and his mates ran to the top of the hill and watched the beautiful old palace burn to the ground. Flames shot hundreds of feet into the sky and it lit up a huge area of London. Over 400 firemen could do nothing to stop its destruction. Among the crowds was Winston Churchill who muttered, "This is the end of an age."

Crystal Palace burning in 1936

By 1937 Norman had saved up seven pounds which was enough money to buy the Hetchins from Dixon, for half its original price. From then on Norman used it daily after his work in the city. He would dodge all the taxis and carts off to their evenings work, and cycle through the streets and sometimes out into the countryside to see what was going on. However cycling through London in winter was another matter.

The poor roads of 1930's London were part pot-hole part cobblestones and a little smooth tarmac. His dad coughed-up the three-pound season ticket to get him to work. He took the 8.17 morning train from Sydenham Penge East to Holborn Viaduct, so that he did not have to risk his life each day riding to work through London in the icy winter months. The three pounds that he paid for Norman's ticket was just one of the many ways his dad helped over the years.

Norman's Hetchins was his pride and joy, to be polished and oiled. Little did Norman guess that seven decades later he would still have his bicycle!

*****

Hetchins bicycles were the iconic British bicycles, and I must add a little chapter about them in case they are lost in time.

The fastest man alive on a self-powered bicycle in 1936 was the German, Toni Merkens. He rode into the halls of fame during the 1936 Olympic Championship in Berlin, watched over by Adolf Hitler. Toni received the gold medal for the men's 1000 meter match sprint event, riding a Hetchins. It was the same Olympics in which Jesse Owens, wearing new Adidas trainers excelled, winning, much to Hitler's disgust, four gold medals.

Norman's curly-stay 1935 Hetchins, still a superb racer today. Note the wiggly back stays for strength and comfort.

Interestingly, Hetchins Bicycles only came into existence because of the Russian Revolution.

Hyman Hetchins 'Harry' and his sister had fled Russia after their parents were killed in the Revolution. On arriving in Britain Harry established a music shop in Leyton. Harry was a keen cyclist and so part of his shop was also selling bicycles.

Harry was joined by an expert bicycle frame builder called Jack Denny. Now, some cyclists of that period had accidents due to the snapping of super-lightweight bike frames as frame builders kept trying to make their racing bikes lighter and lighter. All Hetchins frames were made with the best steel tubing available at the time which was Reynolds 531. It has only recently been superseded by special aluminium and titanium.

Up to the 1930's, just before the mass invasion of the motorcar, the bicycle ruled supreme. Over a million bicycles a year were being built across the country from London to Coventry. Whole suburbs popped up as people could cycle further to work each day. Races like the Tour De France kept the public transfixed by the amazingly versatile invention.

The first road signs were not for cars but for bicycles warning them of the dangers of a steep hill or bend. In the evenings road races were at their height. In London races took place over the bad roads, many Victorian. The rattling and shaking resulted in, not only broken frames but wasted time and speed and plenty of sore bums! "I tell you Alex," said Norman rubbing his backside. "You have no idea how much we tried to cut down on the bikes to make them lighter and faster. The saddles got smaller and smaller until they were little more than a blade of leather. I can feel the bruises now. When you are racing you don't have time to avoid many of the potholes, you are peddling as fast as you can keeping an eye on the cyclist coming up behind and, if you have time, trying to avoid the horse muck."

Jack Denny, the frame builder, believed he could develop a curved frame that would soak up some of the road shocks. He made weird looking curly stays on the rear of the Hetchins frame that absorbed the shocks and even made the bikes more comfortable to ride.

After Toni Merkens won on a Hetchins at the Olympics, the Hetchins name became synonymous with the best money could buy, and every boy-racer dreamed of owning one.

*****

It took Norman nearly eight months to save, scrimping and scraping, but in the end he got his bike. A bike that would stay with him through thick and thin until one summer's day as he walked with me! I'll tell you about that later.

At the weekends, because Norman had only paid for six-day-week lodgings, he would cycle home to St Neots for mum's roast beef and Yorkshire pudding. St Neots was 64 miles from his digs in London!

He worked all week including Saturday mornings at Zurich and every Saturday afternoon Norman would set off on the long cycle journey home with a thermos and packed lunch. Luckily one of his colleagues at the hostel lived in Kimbolton, so Norman and Freddy Wilson would set off on the 128 mile round trip together.

They would head north via Camberwell, across Tower Bridge, Marylebone, Hampstead, up the Edgware Road and into the suburbs of London and then out along the A1 dodging traffic as they went. Because they could go anywhere with their bikes Norman and

Freddy eventually knew every shortcut between London and home. They would take turns in the lead to break the wind, 20 minutes each then switching. Norman's Hetchins had the latest derailleur gears with three speeds! Riding up the A1 they would drop onto the B1428 following the ancient Great North Road to home. Norman would wave goodbye to Freddy as he swung off towards St Neots, always shouting a time to meet up on Sunday to make the return trip.

Hilda, his mum, and the most loving person Norman had ever known, would have his dinner ready and after a good night's sleep and a filling Sunday lunch, Norman would climb back onto his trusty Hetchins to make the long journey back to London. His dad would slap him on the back, "Go on son," Ernest would shout to him as he peddled down the road. "Set a new record to London."

Come rain or shine most weekends Norman made the 128 miles round-journey.

After work at Zurich, with hardly a penny to his name, Norman found that there was not much cheap fun to be had, so he and a few friends from the hostel formed a racing team of their own. There were loads of cyclists at the time and many formed small clubs that survive to this day. Races were regularly held with matches against different clubs and teams. Norman and his pals were as fit as a butcher's dog. "I'll tell you Alex it's probably why I'm still here today at 91. All that exercise did me a lot of good in my youth."

His team would set up time trials and race around London and Kent as fast as their legs would go. Norman became quite a racer during these 'burn-up's' and set a new record among his group on his Hetchins for the 30 mile sprint, officially timed at 87 minutes. Not since Norman had taken a boxing medal at Kimbolton was he so proud. At his old school the tiny terror had been four-stone seven-pounds of pure fighting machine.

It was during one of these "burn-up's' that Norman came a cropper. He was racing full speed down the steep Salt Box Hill near Biggin Hill peddling with all his might, with tears streaming down his face, when a gear slipped and Norman fell onto the handlebars of the Hetchins. On such a steep hill he soon lost control and went tumbling off the bike. The bike was hardly scratched and survived reasonably well with a buckled wheel, but Norman was cut and bruised all over with gravel rash on both legs and a cracked elbow joint. He lay on the ground groaning in agony until he was carted off to hospital.

"You're a lucky lad only breaking your elbow." Said the nurse bandaging him up.

"I don't feel lucky!" Norman mumbled as she carried on.

The landlord who ran his hostel got an urgent message from one of the other lads and came out in his tiny three-wheeled Aero Morgan, and strapped Norman's beloved Hetchins onto the bonnet of his car, and took it back to Sydenham. Norman went to work for a month in a sling.

Along with his cycling Norman found that his evenings raced by in London. He never dreamed of drinking or girls, he never had the spare cash or time for either and it didn't bother him. However Norman did find God one day on his way home from work when he heard a charismatic preacher who drew large crowds at Holborn Viaduct City Temple.

Leslie Weatherhead was a Methodist minister and Christian theologian who had a different approach to preaching and was controversial, questioning many pillars of the Christian faith. Rather than throwing huge lumps of sermon at his flock he used plain talk that they could empathise with. He sympathised with and engaged with his members. He would relate many of the biblical problems of the past to current and topical issues of the day. It was a breath of fresh air for Norman, who had regularly put up with the daily slog at Kimbolton School of morning and evening prayer, and stuffy Sunday school preaching.

Some weekends when Norman had the spare cash for the extra nights lodgings and did not make the long trip home he would go and listen to the preacher and his astounding interpretation of the bible.

And so Norman's life settled down and was taking a steady course. However Hitler had other plans for the young man from St Neots.

Chapter 5 War

By 1939 the Summer Olympics, a few years earlier, had long been forgotten and the team spirit of nations had turned to war. Hitler's unstoppable armies were marching across Europe in their jack-boots with thunder and menace. On September 3rd 1939 Norman was glued to his thermomic-valve radio sipping tea as he heard the powerful words that would change his world. Neville Chamberlain declared *"I have to tell you that this country is at war with Germany. You can imagine what a bitter blow it is to me that all my long struggle to win peace has failed"*

Shortly after all cinemas, theatres and places of entertainment were officially closed.

Enlist Today!

Norman was buzzing with excitement as he went to work with his new tin hat and gas mask. He was about to voluntarily enlist when in early 1940, his 'Call up' papers to the armed forces arrived. As rationing started for the first time in Britain, Norman jumped on his Hetchins and raced to his enrolment office. Norman was lucky, because he had enlisted early, he was given a choice of which force he would like to join. After queuing for an hour a burly sergeant shouted at him "What force laddy?" Quick-as-a-flash and without too much thought Norman shouted back, "Navy please Sir." And that was that. Once more Norman would be close to water.

On April Fool's day 1940, Norman found himself at an old converted Butlins holiday camp at Skegness for naval training. The last time he had been in Skegness was as a child with his dad paddling in the sea. Now he was back to prepare for war.

The camp was renamed HMS *Royal Arthur* and, to begin with, all seemed quite pleasant as the recruits settled in to their huts. But that soon changed. It was the lull before the storm.

He had become an HO—Hostilities Only—ordinary seaman, the lowest of the low in the Royal Navy. Norman was dragged out of bed each morning by the camp bugle. In the yard, come rain or shine, it was exercise and training. After a few weeks Norman got used to the regimented square bashing and monotonous routine.

When he first arrived and was putting his kit away, an officer came in to the barracks to talk to the new recruits. He made it absolutely clear that the petty officer in charge of drills was God, and to cross him was often painful. He told them of a little incident to explain.

One batch of new recruits, all keen and cockey lined up on the parade ground for their first inspection. The officer, a burly powerful man with a voice that could raise the dead, moved along the row prodding and pushing with his stick. "What's your name Charlie Boy?" He bellowed, poking one of the young recruits with his stick.

"Smith sir."

"Smith, Smith. I just called you Charlie, now I'll ask you again. What's your name?"

"Charlie sir." The young lad shouted back.

"Better." The officer huffed and moved on to one bright-eyed lad. He poked him with the stick. "See this stick 'ere Charlie boy? There's a bit of shit on the end of it." Quick as a flash the young lad shouted, "Not on this end sir."

The whole parade ground burst out laughing. However 10 miles later, running in the rain and missing lunch, while the officer screamed at them, it didn't seem quite so funny.

Norman in his first naval uniform at the naval training camp HMS *Royal Arthur,* Skegness.

Norman and the recruits took that message on board and never gave any officer trouble. He was issued with his 'Housewife's kit' a small round tin full of sewing bits for the repair of his uniform. Square bashing each day replaced Norman's exercise on his beloved Hetchins. This disciplinary training gave Norman 'Housemaid's Knee,' a painful affliction from stamping on the parade ground hour after hour. A problem that stayed with Norman all his life.

After a period of training, time came for Norman's first evening's leave into Skegness. News had come through to the camp that the cinemas, theatres and entertainment halls had reopened. They were needed to promote the government propaganda for the war effort.

Norman excitedly joined the queue for his exit permit. As the queue got smaller and smaller he noticed that the exit permit seemed to be rather a funny shape. He stared hard as he got close. After queuing for ages to get his permit he saw that he was not in the queue for permits at all but he was actually in the queue for condoms! Norman coughed, turned red, mumbled something to his mates in the queue, and made a quick exit, heading for the cinema on his own.

At the cinema Pathé news was showing the full horror of war. Also it showed Norman how vital the Navy was to our little island,

and how every man and women should do their part. There was a clip about the Dutch Royal family being rescued from the Nazis at the last moment by a British destroyer, and newsreels from the beaches of France where our retreating army was trapped and desperately waiting for rescue by sea.

Hammock training at Skegness between the Butlins chalets. It would come in handy for Norman getting his hammock up in the dark on a swaying ship.

British Pathé news kept the cinema goers informed of all the war information that the government would allow. All through the war they reported in a very patriotic way with posh cut-glass commentary to go along with all the action. They brought the war in foreign lands alive to all those at home. They mixed the war news with the *Home Front*, also fashion with glamour and film stars sprinkled throughout, filling the cinemas with images of defiant humour, everyone doing their bit for King and Country. The news reels captured the British spirit in the heat of the action and whatever they were filming, be it sport, movie stars or war, the newsreels were always accompanied by stirring patriotic music.

The papers were also full of the terrible news of the trapped soldiers, as the great Battle of Dunkirk raged on the French coast.

Hundreds of thousands of retreating men were trapped on a patch of shoreline as the mighty German army moved in for the kill.

By June of 1940 Norman read of the amazing escape of so many of the Allied forces, and a huge feeling of pride spread among the sailors who had made the impossible a reality. Norman and the crew chatted quietly about events but never openly or loudly. Government officials and spies were supposed to be everywhere and the watch words were always *"loose lips sink ships."*

Norman with his classmates at the converted Butlins, Skegness 1940

Chapter 6
Disaster at sea

After weeks of training Norman was posted for a further six weeks to Chatham Docks, then to his first real ship moored along the Mersey in Liverpool.

As the Royal Air Force was fighting a deadly battle in the skies over southern England that would later become known as the Battle of Britain, a voyage followed for Norman. He set sail on the ill-fated day of Friday the 13th September 1940 into the Battle of the Atlantic. Friday the 13th was traditionally never a day that sailors went to sea but in times of war there was no option.

Friday was traditionally unlucky in the Navy. To combat the reluctance by sailors to go to sea on a Friday a vessel was especially commissioned called HMS *Friday*. Her keel was laid down on a Friday; she was launched on a Friday, commissioned on a Friday and set out for her sea-trials on a Friday. She sank on her maiden voyage!

Norman was posted to *"a bucket'* as he called it that had been refitted to carry troops. It was an outdated vessel but along with other new recruits, they boarded the aging hulks. Their kit and hammocks were thrown in a huge pile on deck, so the first few hours were spent trying to find their own numbered kit and then trying to grab a space to put up their hammocks for the night. All of the experiences and noises onboard Norman's first real ship were exciting, wandering around endless passages trying to find *"the heads'*, or toilets, or the *"mess hall'* where he could get a bite to eat, and then trying to remember the maze of passageways to get back to where he had strung up his hammock.

Convoy OB213, consisting of 19 ships, slowly raised anchor and headed out of Liverpool along the River Mersey into Liverpool Bay, and then the Irish Sea. The lumbering goliaths pointed their bows toward Canada and blackened the air with their smoke. They were off to Nova Scotia and Quebec to pick up more American destroyers. His ship was crammed with enough extra crew for eight more ships which they would be picking up.

Norman's war had started. Among the flotilla was the *City of Benares* carrying children. Norman waved to the excited kids as the ships went by each other, and spread into a line heading for the horizon.

The destroyers wallowed in the heavy seas across the Atlantic and all the new lads, fresh from training camps, spent a lot of time turning green and leaning over the sides of the ships, throwing up their meals and praying for their sea legs. This was much to the amusement of the old sea-dogs who regularly placed bets on which new recruit would throw up first after leaving the mess hall.

In the evening the older sailors played cards and sang local Liverpool songs.

Oh Maggie May, Maggie May, They've taken you away, To die on Van Diemen's shore, Cause you robbed so many sailors- Captains and whalers, Now you'll never dance down- Lime Street any more.

The convoy kept a keen eye out for the German U-boats that silently stalked the depths looking for easy prey. The children on the *City of Benares*, just one ship behind Norman's, were being evacuated to the safety of Canada. Homes had been arranged for them and families were waiting.

The Children's Overseas Reception Board had carried out several mass evacuations of children out of harm's way. The Blitz in London was killing one-in-ten children and as many children as possible were being moved out of the reach of Goering's lethal Luftwaffe. Telegrams were usually sent from Canada House in London telling the lucky parents when and where the ships were leaving. Parents took their children to the docks and bravely waved them off to a safer life away from the bombings. In the parents hearts a desperate choice had to be made. To their children's faces they acted out a fantasy of brief enjoyable holidays and far away adventures, but as their faces turned away on the dockside the tears fell.

Getting the children on board ship was one problem but getting across the deadly seas was another.

Six hundred miles out at sea HMS *Winchelsea* and two sloops left to join another eastbound convoy. The remaining ships ploughed on toward the Canadian coast. Orders had been given to disperse the convoy as they were easier to spot in a large group. The orders also contained instructions in case of attack. If a ship is attacked do not congregate or attend the ship that has been hit or your vessel will become another target, carry on regardless of what happens. The ships moved apart but some still kept within visual communication distance in case of trouble. Little did they know that these precautions would be of no use. In the rough North Atlantic waves, death was waiting.

Stalking the convoy was a lone wolf. Under the water with just the periscope showing was one of the most deadly U-boats of the Second World War, U-48. The U-Boats usually hunted in groups known as 'Wolfpacks,' stalking by day and attacking at night, but the deadly U-48 was a loner. The German submariners called the shadowing of their prey, "rabbit hunts'. During the war the underwater devil sank at least 55 allied ships and took thousands of lives. Many of the crew proudly wore Iron Crosses for their terrible work. Back in Germany they were treated like conquering heroes and hailed as champions glorifying in the death of so many lives.

No one has ever properly explained why a nation became obsessed with dominating the entire world. No one explained how German parents would kiss their own children goodbye and then go and kill others. It was like a mass hypnotic hysteria brought on by a few charismatic lunatics. Throughout the war atrocities became common, though the media tried to hide many of them.

Although the City of Benares had clearly been designated as a refugee ship she was being stalked. Had Norman's ship been a little slower or the U-Boat a little faster their ship would be the one that was being hunted.

Little did the children onboard know that during the night as they finished their letters to their parents and went to bed, torpedoes were piercing the water towards them. Over a period of hours several torpedoes missed, but at a minute after midnight on the 18th September the U-boat came up really close and fired two more directly at the City of Benares before slipping back in to the black murky depths. The ship, only four years old, took a direct hit to the stern and started to sink almost immediately.

The damage to the City of Benares was devastating, and orders were given, by the master Captain Landles Nicoll, to abandon ship. The children were evacuated first but in the stormy seas several lifeboats capsized and in the ensuing dramatic struggle for survival over half the 406 adults and most of the children lost their lives.

HMS *Hurricane*, with no thought to her own safety, managed to rescue over 100, but of the 90 children only seven survived. However on the 25th September an S-25 Sunderland flying boat on a routine mission spotted a craft adrift 600 miles from land. A second plane dropped supplies and HMS *Anthony* was told of their location. She picked up the small group of survivors who had drifted for eight days in the lifeboat. There were six more children aboard.

Captain Nicoll was not among the survivors. He had organised what he could and like many great captains had gone down with his ship. However brave women like Mary Cornish, a music teacher, were aboard. She had done her utmost to rescue the children while the *City of Benares* was going down. She was later decorated for bravery.

After the tragedy the Overseas Reception Board changed their strategy of sending children abroad, so that the heartbreak could never be repeated.

*****

America was Britain's lifeline during the war and Commander of the German U-Boat's, Karl Dönitz, knew this all to well. His orders were clear and simple, destroy all Allied shipping. The Germans were so successful that early on in the Battle of the Atlantic they were sinking nearly 50% of all Allied shipping. The losses were disastrous and kept secret from the worrying public. Over 30,000 seamen went down with their vessels. The fuel tankers were the worst. Easy pickings for the U-Boats they were slow, large and cumbersome and when hit they exploded and set the surrounding sea alight. Few crew escaped alive.

Convoys shuttled constantly between America and Britain escorted by as many armed naval vessels as possible but they were at a disadvantage to the U-Boats stalking them. The Germans waited in their "*Wolfpacks*' around the mid Atlantic at designated MOMP or Mid Ocean Meeting Points, where the American escort ships would take over from the British and vice-versa. The U-Boats stretched out, constantly searching for signs of Allied shipping. When one was spotted they signalled the other submarines and converged on the convoy. They would wait till nightfall before moving in for the kill.

The War Cabinet was alarmed and poured huge resources into producing equipment to deal with the menace that could lose Britain the war. At one point the Germans were sinking over 50,000 tonnes of shipping a month. In 1940 the Germans sunk over two million tonnes of shipping. Norman was in the middle of the worst struggle for survival that had ever faced the Royal Navy. Churchill spoke words of encouragement to the men, "*I have complete confidence in the Royal Navy. I am sure they will be able to meet every changing phase of this truly mortal struggle.*"

However U-48 was not done. After sinking the *City of Benares* they joined their dreaded '*Wolfpack*' and hunted down convoy SC-7 coming the other way from Nova Scotia. In the ensuing struggle they sank 20 of the 35 cargo vessels bound for Britain and Liverpool.

Luckily the tide of German U-Boat supremacy slowly turned as Britain improved their U-Boat hunting capabilities and their depth charges. They also developed ASDIC the equivalent to the American sonar and fast reaction long range bombers. The deadly U-Boats, so successful during the early part of the war, went from the hunters to the hunted. The U-Boats who had so callously named their foe '*Rabbits*' found that the rabbits bit back. Over 60% of all frontline U-Boats were eventually sunk.

*****

Norman's convoy was still desperately making for Halifax. Eventually they made it safely into port. The British forces were under strict instructions to be upbeat and enthusiastic to the Canadians. They were to encourage volunteers and to be positive for the waiting Canadian press. No mention was to be made of the terrible tragedies that were taking place in the cold Atlantic waters.

The crews did exactly what the British do best. They arrived in Halifax with much pomp and circumstance. Norman and the rest of the lads put on their best uniforms and marched down the main street of Halifax with the ship's band bashing out the tune *Roll out the Barrel*. The marching men had tears in their eyes from their bitter experience in the Atlantic, but, to the Canadians that cheered them all down Main Street, all was well.

The crew of the ships carrying them to Halifax then did the same thing as they had done before in Liverpool, dumping all the new-boys kit into a pile on the quayside. The kit was then thrown onto trucks and taken to a stadium in the centre of Halifax that had been converted into dormitories for the new arrivals. The trucks then made yet another pile of their kit and drove away laughing. Norman and his fellow sailors shouted a few good old British words of encouragement as they left, shrugged their shoulders and got stuck into the tedious job of identifying their own kit. By night-fall they had all been fed and settled in.

Norman learned from the shore crew that the destroyers that they had come to pick up had been swapped for some land leases by the Americans. They were pretty obsolete by 1940 but Churchill was desperate for them. Norman was later to find out to his peril that his ship was not only old but also leaked! The foul smell of sea water mixed with fuel oil is a memory indelibly ingrained in Norman.

On the voyage back there were more calamities as the ships ran with their new raw crews. Some of the old sailors made sure that the new young sailors were scared to death. "See that boys, that's Gannet Rock. There's hidden ledges there that'll drag a ship down before you can call fer' yer' mother. I've seen men go down screamin' to

Davy Jones' Locker more than once. My own Pa went down there in 1899 on the *Castillian*."

One of the ships had engine trouble and had to turn back in mid-Atlantic. One stopped at St John's in Newfoundland and would go no further. Two of the ships later collided in Belfast, and eventually only three ships made it to their final destination at Devonport. It seemed that the Germans were doing very well, without having to even be there!

At Devonport the old ships had a quick refit and then up to the Kyle of Lochalsh, Scotland to join the North Atlantic Convoys.

Norman took a shine to navigation and helped the Canadian navigating officer with the Admiralty maps as they toured the northern hemisphere. Norman grew his sea legs, toughened up, and went from a boy to a man on the long convoys which were constantly under attack from German, ships, planes and submarines as well as the natural perils of the sea, of ice and winter storms.

Norman's shift, or watch, was four-hours on four-hours off with two dog-watches. First Watch was eight to midnight, Middle Watch was midnight to four in the morning, Morning Watch was four to eight, Forenoon Watch was eight to midday and Afternoon Watch was midday to four in the afternoon. Then there were the two Dog Watches split around the meal times, First Dog Watch from four to six and Second Dog Watch from six to eight in the evening. Naval tradition called them Dog Watches as you only had time to nap like a dog on a two-hour shift.

Norman carefully learned the navigating techniques and became a navigator's yeoman correcting maps as they rocked over the waves from port to port. He bonded with the crew as they escorted convoy after convoy, sometimes escorting whaling ships or armed merchant ships which were named DEMS or Defensively Equipped Merchant Ships.

They ploughed the cold waters of the north along the great circular route picking up and delivering supplies from ports like Murmansk. Then off to Reykjavik in Iceland and the frozen coasts of Greenland, cutting under the Arctic Circle to Canada. Sometimes the sea was so rough the ships were tossed around like toys in a bath, and sometimes the sea almost froze and great icebergs drifted by. Occasionally the Northern Lights would light up the night sky and flickered like green diamonds creating mesmerising displays. On those magical nights it seemed almost like heaven would come down and kiss the sea.

The ships would often pull into different ports and leave was given. The crew would wander off looking for something to do in the strange lands. On one of these shore leaves near the Isle of Skye Norman came across a local farmer trying to free a lamb stuck in a hole. Norman quickly rolled up his sleeves and dived in helping where he could and soon the beast was freed, bleating as it ran off.

When Norman stood up to rub some of the mud off him he looked closer at the farmer only to see it was actually the Admiral of the Fleet in civvies! Not the usual formal meeting for an admiral but they walked back to base together, chatting as they went.

What Norman had not realised is that during his sea voyages the navigating officer had been keeping a close eye on him and had recommended Norman for officer training. He could see the potential in the young seaman with his quick wit, ability to learn and sea-skills. Norman also had another ability that was essential in all good officers, men trusted and respected him.

After Norman's last Atlantic Convoy, before officer training, he was sent to Devonport. Gone with the Wind was showing at the 'Flicks' with the gorgeous Vivien Leigh and Olivia de Havilland. An evening watching the American Civil War with Clark Gable would take anyone's mind off what was happening. The film, which scooped 10 Academy Awards, showed almost non-stop for four years to heaving audiences. Even during the Blitz in London the Cinemas were jam-packed.

Norman spent a while on, or as the Navy say, in HMS *Meynell*, a Hunter class escort destroyer that had duties all along the coast from Sheerness to Scapa Flow. The Meynell was named after the old Derbyshire hunt, and for a period was equipped with an improved highly secret anti-submarine detection device called ASDIC. This allowed the ship to detect the unseen enemy and give chase.

Chapter 7
Officer training

Norman's next chapter in his war was to attend officer training at the imposing Lancing College. Norman had made his first step up the naval ladder and was now a "Snottie'. The term used for the young officers came from their uniform which had extra buttons on the sleeves to remind the new officers to stop wiping their noses with their sleeves out at sea. Okay for the sailors but quite unbefitting for a naval officer!

He felt like he was driving into a film set as the truck dropped a gear and chugged up the hill towards the college. Its towering gothic revival chapel jabbed at the sky with its high towers and dominated the surrounding Sussex skyline. The college had been requisitioned by the Navy and renamed HMS *King Alfred*. It was a shore training station known by the men as a stone frigate or a concrete carrier as it was far from the sea.

Lancing College in the background was renamed HMS *King Alfred* and known as a stone frigate as it was not on the sea.

Thousands of prospective officers, both men and women of all classes, trained at Lancing. Many of the new recruits had little or no sea experience at all so everything was new to them. The classes were long and hard and often interrupted with air raid sirens. As soon as the sirens sounded everyone moved off in orderly fashion to their allotted bunkers or basements. However when the planes got too close they all ran like crazy for cover.

Norman gained a white band around his cap which showed he was training as an officer. He moved between HMS *King Alfred* and the docks at Hove and Shoreham on the shore where they carried out practical training and drills on real ships.

Norman was one step ahead of many of his colleagues as he had already experienced war and some of the harshest conditions known to sailors on the High Seas. His experience was welcomed by his fellow officers-in-training and together they worked hard and learnt fast.

HMS *King Alfred* was a breeze for Norman who had survived the frostbitten waters of the north where the storms could rip your ears clean off. Most evenings an old crate would turn up at the college nicknamed the liberty bus. The bus went straight into Brighton. Brighton was the hottest nightspot in the country after London, and clubs and pubs stayed open late to entertain the servicemen and women from all around the area. Any spare cash was blown on drink and dancing before the mad rush to catch the last bus back to base. If you missed the bus it was a long walk through the night and a reprimand if you didn't manage to sneak in without being seen.

Being near the coast, a port and an airbase was no picnic. Brighton and Shoreham were not far from the enemy flight-path to London. Many times the loud wailing of the air raid sirens would send people running for the nearest shelters. German planes, returning from raids, with ammunition left over would drop their bombs on the towns and strafe the streets with their last bullets before heading back over the coast. They seemed to take joy in chasing anything that moved and trying to kill it, including the cattle which were shot at Applesham Farm near Lancing. Taking advantage of the slaughter, dearly-rationed beef was suddenly available to all the locals for nearly a week.

After a final inspection at Lancing, by King George VI, Norman was passed out as an officer. King George was a naval man through-and-through. He had served on board HMS *Collington* at the battle of Jutland in 1916, during the First World War. Unlike his public reserve, in action the King was a fearless fighter and was mentioned in despatches for his bravery.

King George was a reluctant king and painfully shy, he was almost the complete opposite of what a public servant should be. Years earlier the young Prince had cried his heart out when he had heard the news that he was to become king on his brother's abdication. He took some consolation in believing that it was his fate and that he was being guided by a spiritual presence. Even at his coronation to become King George VI he said privately that he would never have been able to get through the day without help from above.

King George VI inspecting Norman and his fellow officers at HMS
King Alfred

The King's public stammering gave onlookers the false
impression that he was weak but behind his frailty in public was a
steely determination and devotion to his country. In private or when
he was at ease he was high spirited and loved to fool around, sing
songs and make up stories for his children, the little princesses.

Before he was King he had spent years in therapy to help reduce
his nervous stammer that was dominating his public appearances.
Nothing had helped until the Australian born therapist Lionel Logue
worked his magic on the King at his shabby Harley Street office.

Along with 10,000,000 listeners Lionel Logue had seen Albert's
inaugural public speech, as the Duke of York, at the British Empire

Exhibition at Wembley in the 1920's. His father, King George V, had pushed his son hard in the mistaken belief that if he threw him into the deep end he would learn to swim.

It was a disastrous idea that led to the future king of England suffering terribly from stomach ulcers. Lionel had felt his pain as the Duke stammered and stuttered, stumbling heartbreakingly through his words. Lionel knew he could help the young man, and when the chance arrived he transformed Albert's ability to control his nerves when speaking in public.

They formed a great bond and Lionel or 'Liney,' almost became the father figure that Albert had longed for as a lonely child. Lionel was besides the King for nearly every one of his wartime speeches. In recognition of the King's gratitude he made the brilliant therapist a Commander of the Royal Victorian Order. The pair stayed firm friends throughout their lives, both dying within a year of each other.

By the time Norman met the King at Lancing he projected a confident and powerful figure. He spoke to Norman and his fellow officers without a hint of a stutter.

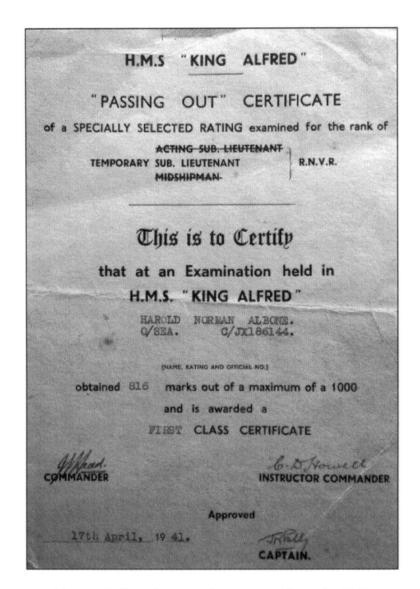

H.M.S "KING ALFRED"

"PASSING OUT" CERTIFICATE

of a SPECIALLY SELECTED RATING examined for the rank of

~~ACTING SUB. LIEUTENANT~~
TEMPORARY SUB. LIEUTENANT   R.N.V.R.
~~MIDSHIPMAN~~

This is to Certify

that at an Examination held in

H.M.S. "KING ALFRED"

HAROLD   NORMAN   ALBONE.
C/SEA.   C/JX186144.

[NAME, RATING AND OFFICIAL NO.]

obtained 816   marks out of a maximum of a 1000

and is awarded a

FIRST CLASS CERTIFICATE

COMMANDER   INSTRUCTOR COMMANDER

Approved

17th April, 19 41,

CAPTAIN.

Norman's first class passing out certificate in 1941

Throughout the war, King George VI and his queen, Lady Elizabeth Bowes-Lyon, worked tirelessly to stabilise the throne and the country. Prince Albert, Bertie to his friends, had fallen in love with Elizabeth after a debutante's ball at Buckingham Palace. He was persistent with his amorous attentions towards Elizabeth. He swore that if he did not marry her, he would never marry anyone. She eventually gave in to him and said yes on his third attempt. They married in one of the first big public Royal weddings. During the war their unbounded passion for the people and morale boosting journeys all around the country, and abroad, helped improve spirits and filled the British people with determination.

Unfortunately King George still smoked relentlessly and quietly drank to help steady his nerves; sadly both would later contribute to his early death.

Norman, top row middle, and his fellow officers at HMS *King Alfred*

There was no grand passing out parade on becoming an officer for Norman or his fellow colleagues, just a few days leave. Britain was at war and they had to get down to business. Norman was issued with his officer's uniform and cap. His cap came in a tin for protection called a "*Ditty Tin*'. The tin was just big enough for a few personal effects and would travel with him all over the world.

Chapter 8

When Norman was asked if he had any preferences to his posting he decided that, because he had known destroyers, a posting on another destroyer would be the ticket.

He was commissioned as sub-lieutenant with a gold band on his sleeve, given his posting and a weekend's leave. He had not yet told his parents the news that the ordinary seaman had now become a commissioned officer. His first stop on leave was to rush home in his officer's uniform.

Norman felt like a King travelling on the trains with everyone looking at him. His mum leapt for joy and flung her arms around him, and started crying with so much pride Norman thought she would take his very breath away. Ernest shook his hand so hard it almost fell off. They wanted to march Norman up and down St Neots High Street all afternoon but Norman persuaded them that he needed a good cup of tea and a sit down.

When it came time for Norman to leave, his mum would not let him go, she just hugged and hugged him. What Norman never knew was that his mum was suffering from terminal cancer.

There was a last minute operation but Hilda died shortly after Norman's visit.

Ernest had to break the hard news to Norman that his mum had died. It was a terrible shock to the 20 year old lad.

I know my son what you are forced to face
A pain that rips your heart.
But be strong for me in love's embrace
For our spirits will never part.

Although Norman was heartbroken, there was little time to mourn in war and after the funeral was over he rushed back to his post. Norman now had second thoughts about the cold weeks on the North Atlantic Convoy miles from home. He asked if he could be posted as an officer on a smaller ship where he could stay closer to shore in case his Dad had need of him.

The Admiralty was aware of Norman's situation and found him a position on the Coastal Forces Patrols where he would stay for the remainder of the war.

Norman as a young officer. Just 20 when his father came to him with the news of his mother's death.

Chapter 9

Norman was posted to Fort William in Scotland, for ship-handling courses. Scotland seemed like a wild abandoned place and a bit of a shock for the young officer. However the port and haggis nights, at the officer's mess, which usually ended with terrible hangovers, made up for it. Norman handled all the new training, official and unofficial, with ease, including a perilous trip to the top of Ben Nevis as a drunken prank.

Norman's first active duty as an officer was back down in London on a small 70-footer called an HDML or Harbour Defence Motor Launch. His duty as a second-in-command, sub-lieutenant, was to take orders from his Commanding Officer and see that his men carried them out quickly and efficiently.

In London they would patrol the Thames estuary, mainly at night, and wait in total darkness on the lookout for German craft trying to sneak in to lay mines. Each day as the sun set they would make their way down to the docks with their blackout torches, complete with ration supplied Eveready batteries, climb aboard ship and move out of port.

The heavy diesel engine would rumble away as they made their way to their start position for the night. Then the ship would go to complete blackout stations. All night they would search the water for signs of German activity. The watches were long and bleak and no light was to be shown in case the enemy spotted it and scarpered.

With no time to rest properly on night duty, naps were taken anywhere. Norman was so tired that he did not even unfold his bed behind the settee he fell asleep on!

Norman's launch was fitted out with a variety of lethal weapons, but the worst of all was the Holman Projector.

Norman described this dangerous device in some detail. The Holman Projector was a 4½ foot steel barrel with a round sight on the end into which explosive rounds were dropped. A pneumatic-air system triggered as the round struck the base of the tube. The rounds themselves were metal containers with short-fused Mills Bombs or hand grenades inside. The high-pressure air bottles were supposed to fire fifty rounds each, up to a height of around 600 feet. The rate of fire could reach thirty rounds per minute in the hands of an experienced crew member.

Norman's conduct certificate from his captain in 1942

However the projector was deadly to friend and foe as sometimes the bomb hardly shot a few feet into the air before exploding. It was just as likely to land on deck or blow your own head off as do any damage to the opponent. It soon became nicknamed the *"Harry Tate'* after a stage comedian of the time who took the mickey out of useless stuff.

It was a stop-gap weapon with serious flaws. An improved version of the 'Harry Tate,' sorry, Holman Projector, was developed and a trial to demonstrate the weapon's new versatility was called in Aldershot, Hampshire.

Winston Churchill was not too impressed. Norman told me that Churchill arrived and was waiting to see this new cost-effective and versatile weapon of the future. Unfortunately they all forgot to bring ammunition! Eventually an officer had a brainwave and rushed off returning with several bottles of beer to substitute as the bombs. Much to the onlookers amusement the bottles fired successfully, exploding in a frothy thud on their targets. The Prime Minister later commented, not on the efficiency of the weapon, but the lack of beer over lunch!

Even with the improvements Norman decided not to order the use of the projector unless he and his crew were in an extremely dangerous position.

A few of Norman's crew next to the machine guns with a very young Norman top centre right

After a short period Norman gained his watch-keeping certificate, and the time came to get the launch refitted with more weapons. This entailed a winding trip up the Thames to Teddington Lock. It was quite a journey. Everyone in Britain was on a knife edge watching out for the enemy who were going to appear at any second. For those living along the river the 70 foot motor launch was quite a sight as it rumbled up Old Father Thames. The twisting river trip was an exciting journey with children often running along the riverbanks waving flags. The Home Guard also mustered to take a close look at the launch, just in case it was the enemy making a surprise attack.

Chapter 10

In 1943 Norman moved up to a brand new 112 foot B-class Motor Launch based out of Newhaven on the south coast. Norman and his crew escorted convoys up the coast, mainly under the cover of darkness, passed Dungeness or *'Dungie'* as they called it and around the most dangerous strip of water in the world at the time, the Straits of Dover known as *"Hell's Corner'*.

Here the enemy were in plain sight, often ordering attacks from the air. The convoys would thrust ahead at full steam, round the exposed heel of England's coast, and make for the safety of Ramsgate. A few hours kip followed on-board, then back to sea again to escort another convoy back to Newhaven. It was a dangerous game of cat and mouse with many casualties but the ancient sea route was still considered the easiest way to move goods around the coast.

When time allowed, Norman and his men enjoyed a tipple in port at Ramsgate. Often at the Rising Sun in Effingham Street. On their way to the pub they would lock their arms together striding down the street singing, *"You are my sunshine my only sunshine, you make me happy when skies are grey."*

On one occasion after a few pints with some RAF drinking boys Norman found himself gripping onto the inside of a

Boston bomber as its Wright Cyclone supercharged engines screamed for mercy. From then on Norman restrained himself from asking silly questions of RAF pilots like, how fast does she go?

10, Downing Street,
Whitehall.

30 May, 1943

I have noted with admiration the work of the light coastal forces in the North Sea, in the Channel and more recently in the Mediterranean.

Both in offence and in defence the fighting zeal and the professional skill of officers and men have maintained the great tradition built up by many generations of British seamen.

As our strategy becomes more strongly offensive, the task allotted to the coastal forces will increase in importance, and the area of their operations will widen.

I wish to express my heartfelt congratulations to you all on what you have done in the past, and complete confidence that you will maintain the same high standards until complete victory has been gained over all our enemies.

Winston Churchill

While at Newhaven Norman fell for a local nurse called Gwen and when he had leave they would often whip off to London and stay at the fabulous Berners Hotel just off Oxford Street.

War has that amazing way of bringing people together. Imagine for a second that you were at war, right now! Tomorrow you may be dead, maybe even tonight in the bombings. Few plans were made for next week, or next year, because there was a high chance you would not be here. Each time Norman's ship sailed out of port on another mission it could have been his last.

No one is absolutely positive but we now know that around 70 to 80 million people died during the Second World War. The worst casualties by far being the Soviet Union who lost over 23 million and China, who we hardly even mention when discussing the war, lost over 20 million. If you think about it for a second, if each of those lost souls joined hands they would stretch easily around the entire world.

By 1943 the war was well under way and although the English Channel was a rough and dangerous strip of water, it was never as bad for Norman as the deep wallowing troughs of the Atlantic that he had endured in the early years of war.

Also another benefit of being so close to home was that they had fighter protection in the Channel. From spotting and reporting the enemy to an aircraft reaching it could be as little as 15 minutes. This backup was reassuring to Norman and his band of brothers.

One of the many Costal Convoys being undertaken with another four ships in front of these. Fast German attack-craft would appear out of nowhere, especially when the convoy was near the enemy coast and aircraft would spray the ships with bullets.

Norman was a quick learner and was now a well qualified and trained professional. He had seen service over many seas and many ports, chased E-Boats out of Lowestoft and spent endless nights glued to his binoculars waiting for his foe. Lowestoft was a dangerous estuary. Coming home exhausted from a long tour of duty, when the east wind was blowing across the bay and the tide dragging fast, you had to have your wits about you just to get home safely. Some did not.

Can you imagine for a moment what it was like out at sea on war duty? The cold dark night all around, the ship wallowing up and down with the black waves. The chance of sighting the enemy at any moment meant no lights in case you were spotted. Just the constant vigilance throughout the long dark hours. As the pale dawn slowly grew, back home to port, hoping that the enemy had not snuck around you during the sinister night and placed hidden mines in the mouth of the harbour. Then, at last, once more to sleep.

Any seafarer knows that the sea can be a tempestuous mistress. Sometimes she is calm and clear to the horizon but within hours she can change to a wild tossing cauldron, throwing any ship around like a child's toy in a bath. The sea is devoid of emotion; she'll lure you in, enticing you with a serene quilt of sparkling diamonds and then throw a rage so fierce swallowing man and boy alike with no remorse. Each time Norman's crew made it safely back to port it was not only a success, surviving the enemy, but it was one more test of man against nature.

After more service Norman was recalled to the admiralty. They reviewed his progress in the war so far and promoted him once again. This time it was to a full lieutenant. He was given a brass crest for his officer's cap and two full stripes on his sleeves.

Chapter 11
Harbour Defence Motor Launch 116

Norman had worked his way up from a raw recruit through the ranks all the way to a full-lieutenant and for the first time given full command of his own ship. And what a beauty it was. Norman stayed with his new ship through thick and thin until hostilities ended in Europe.

He became commanding officer on board the sleek HDML116, a brand new 112 foot motor launch with the highest specifications of the day, including radar which, when it worked, was like a gift from the gods. Norman had officers under him now and a crew of 17. He had reached a position every boy dreamed of since the days of Nelson. To be master of his own ship.

Before wireless and radar, communications were minimal, they had semaphore, messages sent with flags by the *"bunting boy'*, and Morse code. There was no picking up the phone and talking. Sparks, the wireless operator would send and receive Morse Code and translate for the officers. During close convoy Morse Code could be sent via flashing lights or heliograph to and from other ships. There were also rules for the sea, a highway code. The lights on board ship signalled which way you were facing and allowed other ships in the dark to know which way you were travelling. The rules were simple, green to green, red to red, all safe to go ahead. Green to red, red to green danger, danger, make sure you're be seen.

Lights were one of the best ways of sending messages when in close convoy at night.

Before radar Norman would be given his orders and would plot a course on his charts. He would take compass bearings and check his watch. A complex calculation using the nautical tables would be used, and during daylight any landmarks were a help. Norman would take a bearing on two landmarks then mark the chart to find his position. From there he could take a compass reading, calculate wind, current and drift then plot a course. When no landmarks were available, a sextant was used to plot the angle of the sun against the time and with the charts a position could be worked out.

All this was complicated and, at night, with no lights and when the searchlights would only pick out the next wave, you sometimes put your faith in God that you could find your way home. There was no substitute for experience and luckily for Norman's crew, he was a master. Norman knew every curve and every spit of land, cliff face and bay in his area. Time after time he could plot a course quickly and accurately and bring his men safely home.

Norman's first full command, the well-armed and fast ML116

Norman only stood five feet four inches in his prime but, like Nelson, his men respected him and gave him their best. His new ship was a smooth, sleek vessel with a low draught for inshore work and powered by two enormous 600 horsepower

Hall Scott Defender V12 engines, it was nimble, fast and could travel 1,500 miles without refuelling.

The Hall Scott engines had overhead cams and updraft carburettors and roared like beasts when under full power. More than 20 knots was not impossible under the right conditions. However 14 knots was a comfortable speed that the engines could maintain for many hours.

The crew relaxing over the ship's cannon before shore leave

The Fairmile Motor Launch HM ML116 was an escort vessel for convoy protection with fast attack capabilities. The launch could also be refitted for minesweeping and mine laying duties. It could be used for coastal raids or as an ambulance launch, also for patrols, and many other duties like harbour defence, submarine chasing and armed high speed air-sea rescue. Several launches were also secretly modified to sweep for acoustic mines and specialised magnetic mines.

The Fairmile came about through clever planning by the admiralty before the war. A flexible craft was needed for many duties and to provide inshore support that the larger vessels could not. Shortly before the Second World War plans were submitted to the Admiralty for a motor launch to be used in action against the enemy.

The launch was designed to use prefabricated parts, which allowed various small manufacturers, such as furniture manufacturers, shipwrights and boat builders to produce individual components. These components could then be assembled in separate shipyards all around the country and in fact the world.

Convoy duty through the English Channel. Any second the enemy could appear.

Although painted 'Admiralty Grey' the hull was made of mahogany planking with plywood frames, which divided the ship into watertight compartments. This was to come in very handy for Norman shortly after he gained command.

All the launches were essentially the same, although they could be adapted to serve in many different roles as they had pre-drilled rails on their decks to allow for various armaments.

Their main armament reflected their anti-submarine and fast attack focus. They had 12 depth charges, one set of twin 0.303 inch machine guns and a single 3 lb gun aft. Norman had a 6 lb gun on the bow and Oerlikon 20 mm cannon on either side of the armour-plated bridge. To add to this they had two 0.303 Lewis Automatic Machine Guns and smoke mortars. Basically they were armed to the teeth and regular practice made perfect.

It was also common to carry hand grenades on the bridge for close-quarter work with the enemy. These launches became so useful in the Navy that they were affectionately known as the Navy's 'Little Ships' and had a huge impact on the outcome of the war.

The launches proved themselves to have excellent sea-keeping qualities in most weather conditions, although there was a tendency towards broaching in high seas if hit side-on by large waves. In almost all weathers including Force Eight, and above, the craft, although thrown about by the sea and continually covered in spray still maintained their buoyancy and carried out their duties.

These British Coastal Craft operated mainly in the English Channel and North Seas, especially in the build up to the Normandy invasion of 1944. In total, the Navy's *"Little Ships'* manned by men with stout hearts and strong wills sank 797 enemy vessels, including 33 midget submarines and 48 E-boats and fought over 781 actions. They fired over 1000 torpedoes, shot down 32 enemy aircraft and carried out many mine laying and mine sweeping operations.

At least 170 of Norman's *'Little Ships'* were sunk or destroyed during action.

Norman was now based at Devonport which he had known well from his early days on the destroyers. He would receive different orders from the Admiralty most days and carry out convoy duties along the South Coast.

Disaster strikes

One night, in a heavy fog, Norman was carrying out convoy duties around the ill fated *'Hell's Corner'* of Dover. All was going well until the fog became so thick they lost sight of the convoy. Norman was an excellent navigator but in pitch dark, smothered in fog, they slowed to a minimal speed and crept along. The big Hall Scott engines set to slow-ahead rumbling below. Suddenly there was an almighty crunch. In the darkness they had been rammed by another vessel. Was it a German ship? "ALL HANDS ON-DECK, MAN YOUR POSTS," Norman screamed.

Water was rushing into the ship and there was a real fear of sinking. Norman gave the order to shut and brace all watertight doors.

This is where the brilliant build of the ships came into their own. Norman had to make the decision to get to a harbour and quick. However, as the ship moved forward it listed badly and took on more water. With the bow ploughing downward into the sea as they moved it became a life and death situation.

Norman came up with the solution of turning the ship around and travelling astern or backwards. This allowed the ship to slowly make way without taking on too much water.

There was no time to waste. Under the most extreme pressure you could imagine on the wallowing bridge Norman used all his navigation skills to plot a course to the nearest port, Dover. He gave the bearing. The ship was listing badly and ramming backwards into the waves and taking on more water. SOS was sent out by '*Sparks*' but they were running out of time fast.

Listing badly and after what seemed like a lifetime of rumbling backwards in the dark one of the crew spotted a ship and caught their attention with the heliograph light, praying to God that it was friendly. Their luck held and the ship came along side tied up the ML116 and towed Norman's craft backwards the remaining few miles into Dover Harbour.

Had Norman plotted the wrong course, even slightly, they could all have been lost at sea or taken by the enemy just another statistic of war. Much to his crew's delight Norman's lucky streak was still with him.

At Dover temporary repairs were made and as soon as the weather changed they headed for Portslade where the ship was fully repaired in dry dock.

While there, Norman was relieved of command and an enquiry was called. Norman had to appear before the Officer's Hearing and explain his actions. No other British craft reported being damaged. After deliberation by the officers Norman was cleared of all charges, his actions in saving his crew were exemplary and Norman was recommended to resume his command at the earliest opportunity. It was a close shave for Norman and his crew, but once again they had come out unscathed.

Chapter 12

Norman's crew, his small band of brothers that lived, ate and fought together. Norman, second row far right, now lieutenant and commanding officer aboard the ML116.

All through the war Norman happily snapped away with his Agfa Carat 4.5 camera. This was forbidden and highly sensitive material, even publicity propaganda was heavily censored. However because Norman's Dad developed the pictures no one ever found out and Norman naively kept his camera handy taking pictures wherever he went. Had he been caught there would have been all hell to pay. However Norman's personal photographs of the crews that he served with have provided us with unique material of his fighting men never seen before.

By early 1944 Norman's launch was modified once again, this time for its most important duty of the war, but everything was hush-hush and no one knew exactly what was about to happen.

At Shoreham, his craft was fitted with Oropesa minesweeping equipment and the officers and crew were instructed on its use, which was tricky because sweeping for mines with razor wire could easily slice your arm off, and the equipment needed to be handled with great care to avoid a nasty accident.

Oropesa minesweeping was a method of sweeping moored mines with a special wire cable towed by the minesweeper. The long cable was fitted with razor wire and wire cutters along its length, which cut the mines' cables that moored them to the spot. The cutting wire was towed astern of the ML116 with a special kite or block to keep the wire down to a fixed depth below water.

At the far end of the wire was a cylindrical, torpedo shaped, steel float and below it the '*otter*' which was a sort of hollow box with steel planes which forced the wire away from the ship as it was towed through the water. As the ship's cutters came into contact with the wires holding the mines they were cut so that the mines floated to the surface where they could be destroyed.

Much to the alarm of locals, for many years Oropesa floats washed up on beaches and because of their torpedo shape they were mistaken for bombs. Often it was only after they had been blown up by explosives experts with a disappointing thud that it was found they were empty and harmless.

After the special refit Norman was ordered back to Devonport where he continued with his crew carrying out convoy duties. In May 1944 special sealed secret orders came to him from the Admiralty.

Full speed ahead. An ML on sea trials.

When Norman pulled into the ancient smugglers port of Brixham, as instructed, he opened his sealed orders. It became painfully clear why his ML116 had been fitted out with the specialist minesweeping gear. He read with great trepidation that his ship was to be in front of the D-day landings, clearing a path for the main offensive toward Utah Beach near the Cherbourg Peninsular.

The news was electric. The invasion was finally here after years of talk, gossip and planning. His men would be filled with excitement and fear in equal amounts. The Germans were ready and waiting for any attack all along the coast. Norman and his crew were going to have to carry out their job right under the enemy's nose in the harshest conditions imaginable.

There were 36 ML craft designated to sweep the shallow beaches in front of the British and American Forces, before and during the invasion of Normandy. The Navy's *"Little Craft'* were to prove vital in the landings of the Allied Forces and the D-Day invasions that would free Europe.

D-Day and the Normandy landings were quite possibly the most important allied landings in European history. Europe as we know it today exists because of the dramatic events that took place in June of 1944.

Chapter 13
The Normandy landings Part 1

Normandy was chosen for the invasion as it had wide open beaches capable of handling the huge numbers of men and machinery that needed to land. However there were massive drawbacks that had to be investigated first. On the plus side the Germans did not expect the invasion to happen at Normandy. They had built their massive fortifications all along the coasts and the Atlantic Wall was thought to be impenetrable by the Germans. To add to this the British had kept up diversionary tactics, constantly throwing false information to the Germans about their possible invasion points.

Churchill and his advisors had learnt a tragic lesson in the failed Dieppe Raid of 1942 when they tried to take the deep-water port. Thousands of Canadian and British troops came back in body bags because of the impassable German fortifications

I remember talking to an old lady who, as a young girl, ran the cinema at the Tide Mills in-between Seaford and Newhaven, where many of the troops for the Dieppe landings were based.

Happy-go-lucky Canadians who bought cigarettes and ice cream from her went off to war in the belief that they would rid the world of a tyrant. She and her mother waved the men off as they sang songs and swapped jokes, boarding the vessels which would take them the 60 miles from Newhaven to Dieppe.

Within a few hours she saw the bodies start to come back. She cried for a week until there were no more tears left. The cinema never reopened. It was a disaster that should never be repeated.

Slowly information for possible landing points was gathered from all around the coasts of Europe. Churchill finally chose the Normandy Coast for the largest mass landings in history. They had learnt a hard lesson from Dieppe and this time the Allies planned a shock and awe tactic of massive unstoppable force.

The Normandy beaches were not the most obvious or safe, but careful planning would help and one part of the plan was to find out exactly what was underneath the soft Normandy sand. A special team was gathered, and six months before the Normandy landings, a group of Royal Engineers were taken through the cold dark waters and dropped off the coast.

Logan Scott-Bowden led his men as they swam ashore. The tides were so strong they came ashore a mile from their intended beach. They crept along the black beach in the howling wind dropping to the sand as the low searchlights swept the shoreline.

On New Years Eve 1943 Logan and his men dug down into the Normandy sand to find out what was underneath. New Years Eve was the chosen date as it was thought the Germans would be celebrating rather than paying attention. It worked, and an elated team waded back out to their waiting craft, some singing and others shouting "Happy New Year" as they went.

The special Royal Engineer reconnaissance team were so successful with their mission that they were sent back two weeks later, to gather more sand with strict orders not to start singing on the way home!

They discovered that beneath the sand lay the remains of ancient forests that had turned to soft peat bogs. A search around the British coasts was started and very similar beaches to Normandy were found in Norfolk. Training was started for the special vehicles needed for the successful June landings. Logan Scott-Bowden and his team were more men in the long list of forgotten heroes, fighting all over the world that made the Allied mission to overthrow the Third Reich possible.

This time the Allies were taking no chances with attacking ports. They built their own ports and harbours to take with them. Portable Mulberry harbours were constructed and when the invasion started they were dragged over to the French coast. Even today at Arromanche in Northern France you can still see the remains of the great hulks that formed the harbours in the 1944 offensive.

As many tiny details were worked out as possible for the Allied Landings and thousands of men and women worked in the strictest secrecy, planning the amazing mission in the hope that the disastrous consequences of the Dieppe Raid would be avoided. Lessons learnt there would save countless lives in the battle to come. Little did Norman and his crew know they would be among the very men that would kick start part of the heroic fight to free Europe.

Fake armaments were built up along the Norfolk Coast to fool the Germans into thinking that the main attack would be at Calais.

But all the time the southern coasts of Britain were filling up with men and machines. However this was not the first major decoy!

Chapter 14
Operation Mincemeat

We British are masters of deception, and one of the most successful operations of the Second World War was Operation Mincemeat. Later, books were written and films made of the amazing deception that grew from a basement building underneath the War Office in London.

The secretive Section 17M, a combined part of operations unit 30AU (AU standing for Assault Unit), was full of brilliant and devious minds like that of Ian Fleming, later to be immortalised for bringing to life in print the ultimate spy, James Bond. Their deadly agents roamed Europe behind enemy lines throughout the war, causing havoc with numerous acts of sabotage. General Patton, disliking their unaccountable actions, referred to them as a bunch of *"Limey pirates'*. The units were trained by survival and weapons experts from all over the world and became known as '*the ghosts of the battlefield'*. They used the lethal and silent Fairbairn-Sykes double-edged killing knives.

Churchill needed a plan to divert German troops away from Sicily and his southern offensive that was to be the first step prior to Normandy. He approved an audacious plot to '*plant'* a dead marine off the coast of Spain for the Germans to find. The body of a poor Welsh miner's son, who had committed suicide, was obtained from Sir Bentley Purchase who ran the St Pancras Morgue in London. The depressed 34-year old had taken his own life with rat poison, but his painful death was to save thousands of lives. Glyndwr Michael's body would be temporarily reborn as Marine Officer William Martin.

His corpse was supplied with every single piece of paperwork and everyday paraphernalia needed. Gentlemen's underwear, scarce in 1943, was acquired from Oxford University. Love letters were written from his imaginary girlfriend and pictures supplied. Even overdue notices and bus tickets were planted on poor Glyn's body. By early summer the stage was set for a brilliant fake. His frozen body was rushed to Scotland where a submarine was waiting.

Captain William Jewell had secret instructions to drop the body off close to the neutral Spanish port of Huelva, Spain. Although

Spain was neutral it was a hot bed of spies and Huelva had a bumper crop of them. The body was slipped out of the torpedo tube as dawn broke, and drifted toward the shore on the incoming tide. Attached to the dead man's arm, with a standard despatch carrier's chain, was a briefcase containing top secret information. The fake information, contained in a sealed letter, pointed to an imminent attack on Greece, not Sicily.

The planning was so meticulous that in the letter was also a single eyelash that would easily drop out when opened. That was the way that the British Consulate would later know if the Germans had opened the letter.

Also, as all this was happening, diversionary attacks were taking place away from Sicily. Special Operations Officers like Geoffrey Gordon-Creed had been dropped behind enemy lines in Greece to cause general havoc or as Churchill put it, *"To set Europe ablaze."* The dashing major was so successful in his operations that some say Ian Fleming based James Bond's character on him.

A Spanish fisherman spotted the body floating offshore and dragged it to his boat. The plan, months in preparation, started to work. Spies informed Berlin and before long detailed photographs of every single item of the dead man was in front of German Intelligence. They scrutinised every morsel and pronounced the letter to the North African Commander, Sir Harold Alexander, as real! Hitler swallowed the bait, hook, line and sinker. Masses of men and munitions were hastily rushed from other defensive positions to Greece.

On the 10 July 1943, 160,000 Allied troops successfully landed in Sicily, not Greece. Operation Husky was a startling triumph with minimal casualties. General George Patton seemed to almost capture the island by himself, and then came precariously close to destroying his glittering career by slapping a sick soldier.

The sick soldier, Charles Kuhl, was slumped over a chair in one of the evacuation hospital tents that Patton was visiting. As Patton entered the room all that could—stood to attention but Kuhl was so exhausted that he stayed in his chair. At the time no one knew what was the matter with Kuhl! There was the possibility that he was just faking his ailment to get out from duty. When Patton asked him why he was there he mumbled something about being nervous and not being able to take anymore. Patton misinterpreted the situation and assumed the soldier was faking his ailments. Patton could not stomach cowards. He erupted slapping the soldier across the face with his gloves. He then grabbed him by his collar, dragged him to the entrance of the tent and threw him out shouting at the guards, "Don't admit this son-of-a-bitch, send him back to the front line. You hear me you gutless bastard? YOU'RE GOING BACK TO THE FRONT."

It was a serious mistake by Patton who was under unimaginable pressure as his forces attacked the enemy. Later it turned out that Kuhl was not only suffering from nervous exhaustion and battle fatigue but he also had chronic dysentery and malaria! It was amazing that he could stand at all. General Patton sincerely apologised for his handling of Kuhl and went back to what he did best, making sure he never repeated his awful mistake again.

The following step for the Allied Forces was Italy and a foothold in German occupied Europe.

Planning was now well underway for the main assault on Normandy, 11 months down the line.

Chapter 15
The Normandy Landings Part 2

Winston Churchill reviewing the American troops at Winchester just before the Normandy landings.

Only a few days in each month were suitable for launching such a vast but delicate operation. A day near the full moon was best both for illumination during darkness, and for the longer tides to land men and machines close to the shore. The moon would also illuminate navigational landmarks for the crews of the aircraft, gliders and parachutists of the 101st Airborne Division of the US Army. A long tide would provide the deepest possible water to help safe navigation over defensive obstacles, placed by the Germans in the sea off the beaches.

A full moon occurred on the 6 June 1944. Allied Expeditionary Force Supreme Commander, Dwight D. Eisenhower, selected 5 June as the date for the assault. The weather was fine for much of May but by the beginning of June it had deteriorated badly. Norman and his crew waited patiently for their orders to go, constantly watching the weather.

A decision had to be made and Eisenhower was desperate to get his forces across the Channel. Every hour that he delayed his attack it could be discovered, and the Germans would move their scattered armaments to concentrate on Normandy. He was facing the same problem that all the invading forces of England had faced since the time of the Romans, but in reverse.

On 4 June the conditions were still too rough for a safe passage to assault the beaches. The high winds had whipped up the sea, making it near impossible to launch landing craft from larger ships at sea. And to make things worse low clouds and poor visibility would prevent our airmen finding their targets.

Most of the Allied troop convoys were already at sea and were being forced to take shelter along the south coast of Britain. The ports were bursting at the seams. The British coast was alive with ships and troop carriers sheltering in every port and safe-haven. It was as if you could almost walk across from one craft to another as they stretched out mile after mile.

Eisenhower waited and waited, holding up the command to go and checking the weather every hour.

Winston Churchill inspecting operations at Dover.

The next full moon period would be nearly a month away, by which time all surprise could be lost. At a vital meeting on 5 June, Eisenhower's meteorologist forecast a brief weather improvement for the following day.

General Bernard Montgomery and Eisenhower's Chief of Staff General Walter Bedell Smith pleaded with Eisenhower to go ahead with the invasion, but Air Chief Marshal Leigh Mallory was doubtful. Admiral Bertram Ramsay believed that conditions would be marginally favourable. With great hesitation and worry

Eisenhower made his decision and ordered the Normandy invasion to proceed on 6 June.

Meanwhile over on the other coast the Germans believed no invasion would be possible in the poor conditions, which were even worse over north-eastern France. The Allied invasion was faced by

50 divisions of the German Army, partly under the control of the formidable General Erwin Rommel.

Some German troops even stood down, and many officers went away for the weekend. Even Rommel went home to celebrate his wife's birthday. Loads of other commanders were away from their posts at war games. All the while under the cover of darkness the allied forces were slowly making their way across the dark rough seas. All hell was about to break loose on the Normandy beaches.

Chapter 16
The Normandy Landings Part 3

The operation was the largest amphibious invasion of all time and one of the most powerful armadas that has ever sailed. The troops were carried across the Channel by over 195,000 allied naval and Merchant Navy personnel in an assortment of 4,128 ships. Norman's little ML116 was dwarfed by the destroyers and troop carriers that he passed along the coast.

The Normandy landings were codenamed Operation Overlord and Operation Neptune. The shore landings were to commence on Tuesday, 6 June 1944, D-Day, at 6:30am.

As the worst of the weather broke the giant armada rumbled toward the Normandy coast. But there was a lot going on before that and Norman was part of it.

History tells us that the Normandy invasion began with overnight parachute and glider landings, massive air attacks, naval bombardments, and then early morning amphibious landings on five beaches codenamed Juno, Gold, Omaha, Utah, and Sword. This was as well as the Allies sending in three airborne divisions behind enemy lines of around 23,000 American, Canadian and Free French airborne troops shortly after midnight. Their job was to prepare for the main assault by taking strategic points, protecting flanks and by disrupting German communications and retreats.

Before it all happened on a dark stormy night Norman's crew and ships like his started their dangerous tasks. Norman had opened his secret orders the day previously and quietly set about instructing his crew. He went for one final drink with 'Messy' Master, commander of ML117 before boarding for his mission. Norman had sailed close to the wind many times but this time he would be in extreme danger.

Norman called his crew together. "Men we have faced many perilous missions on the sea but now I have to ask you to once more put yourselves in harms way. I cannot tell you the specifics of my briefing but let me say that if each man carries out his duty we will do our best to fulfil our orders and come home once more to the safety of our shores."

Sparky muttered something under his breath and went down to the wireless room to study his code books and the rest of the crew took up their positions.

They pulled out of Brixham and headed along the coast picking up more craft as they went. They hugged the coastline and made their way along toward Portsmouth, by which time a small armada had gathered all with their unique orders.

From Portsmouth the convoy headed out into deep water. Norman looked back at his beloved coastline knowing that it may be the last time he saw it. He looked down from the bridge at his men hard at work and knew they would do their very best for King and Country.

ML 117 Commanded by 'Messy' Masters

The all-important minesweepers were escorted on both sides by motor torpedo boats and other larger destroyers. Protecting these small coastal craft on their vital mission was of utmost magnitude. If they failed the Normandy Landings would grind to a halt.

The seas were heavy with strong blustering winds but there was no turning back. They were the spearhead of the main attack and although several of Norman's crew were suffering badly from seasickness the minesweepers were on their way. Norman's, and the other lighter craft had all been designated beaches to shallow mine sweep, and larger minesweepers were to cover the deeper waters off the French Coast.

Once again diversionary forces had also set off to distract any German craft from the real point of invasion. Norman had received his final farewell message from the commander of the Costal Forces but there was no cheering from the dockside for them when they had slipped quietly into the night and sailed into history.

The beaches where the landings were going to take place along a stretch of the Normandy coast all had to be individually swept, and Norman's designated beach was Utah Beach which was the furthest west of the five beaches. Utah was located at the base of the Cotentin Peninsula, and was added by General Eisenhower at a later stage to the original plans to ensure the early capture of the vital port of Cherbourg.

He had realised that the advance throughout Europe would require vast amounts of equipment and, even with temporary harbours, a major port was needed to handle this traffic in the opening stages of the attack.

Utah Beach was about three miles wide and made up of sandy dunes. The landing at Utah, like the other beaches was scheduled for 6.30 in the morning. The force was mainly made up of the US 4th Infantry Division. The plan for Utah included an airborne drop inland by the US 82nd and 101st Airborne Divisions, starting about 1.30 am. The paratroopers were to be dropped inland to secure the roads and fight their way to Utah Beach, causing as much mayhem as possible along the way.

Norman and his crew, along with the other launches, had made it across the English Channel through the wild dark night and were busy at work before all this began, quietly sweeping the inshore beaches of mines where the larger minesweepers could not go.

In reality it was a suicide mission, directly in the line of fire, but in another stroke of luck for Norman the weather was still awful. The crew might have been suffering from the boiling seas but the overcast heavy skies hid the moonlight and the heavy churning seas drowned out the noise from their engines. Norman and his crew efficiently moved to and fro minesweeping along the shallow Utah Beach.

A full moon, clear skies and no wind would have meant certain death to Norman and his crew. They would have stood out for hours like sitting ducks carrying out their lethal orders.

By 6.30 am, as the main landings began, Norman's most dangerous task of the war was coming to an end. He lifted his officer's cap and wiped his brow. With a great sigh of relief he took one last look at Utah Beach through his binoculars to make sure he had missed nothing, and then gave the orders from the bridge to head out into deeper water well out of the way of the approaching armada. He had been rammed once before and did not relish it happening again so close to the enemy. Norman opened the voice tube from the bridge, "Slow ahead," he commanded as he pointed the bow of the ship toward open water. Soon ML116 started to pick up speed. "Half ahead," Norman continued into the tube, "Full ahead." The bow of the ML lifted into the stormy sea as the powerful engines roared below.

Some fast attack German craft did come out of the harbour as dawn broke. However when they realised what was going on, and seeing the massive invasion force before them, they made a hasty retreat to port and stayed there.

Chapter 17
The Normandy Landings Part 4

The sea-borne landing did not go to plan, just about everything that could go wrong did. Strong currents and wild seas meant that the landing craft drifted off their targets and cloud, high winds and flak meant that the airborne divisions also landed way off mark. Smoke screens were useless in the winds and by 6.30 am it was light enough for the enemy to see everything.

Early on during the main attack the German artillery homed onto one of the lead ships, the USS *Corry* (DD463), a Gleaves class destroyer. One of the heavy rounds had struck amidships and jammed her rudder. All she could do was go round and round in a circle, trying desperately to avoid the massive bombardment coming from the German shore defences. With no smoke screen it was to no avail and at around 6.30am, just as the main armada started to land, she was hit below the water line and started to sink.

The USS *Corry* sunk by enemy fire. Only her mast and flag stayed above water

At first, reports came back that it was a mine that Norman may have missed, but the captain later explained what actually happened. It was a missile barrage from a heavy shore battery that had pinpointed her position once she had run out of steam.

Broken and taking on water the captain ordered all men to abandon ship. One sailor in an act of defiance raised the American flag up the main mast. As the ship sank and settled onto the shallow sea bed some 30 feet below—the top of her mast stayed out of the water. With her flag still flying the main Armada ploughed on by.

Craft ploughing towards the Normandy coast in the greatest armada ever assembled.

The German High Command, still sure Normandy was a decoy, were fixated on Calais as the main area of attack from the Allies. Amazingly, even as D-Day got underway, they carried on moving troops there. Field Marshal Von Rundstedt, who had control over much of the area, was not permitted by Hitler to commit his armoured reserve until it was way too late. There was no massive counter attack.

In truth, whatever he had done, he would have lost.

The years of Allied planning and the enormous size of the military machine involved were almost unstoppable. Von Rundstedt later blamed Rommel and other senior officers for his own failures, but in reality the Allied Forces were in such number and with such overwhelming power of men and machines that, resistance however fierce and costly would have been futile.

Utah beach on the morning of D-Day

As the landing progressed the failing Von Rundstedt was suddenly removed from his command. On 29 June he shouted at Field Marshal Keitel, the Chief of Staff at Hitler's HQ. "Make peace you idiot before it is too late." They were his final words in command.

Chapter 18
The Normandy Landings Part 5

Back on Utah Beach the forces landed a long way from their intended targets. Luckily for them where they did come ashore happened to be one of the lesser-defended areas. Because of this the casualties were much lower than the carnage taking place on some of the other beaches. Even the observation posts attacked at Îles Saint-Marcouf, a couple of hours before the main invasion, turned out to be unoccupied.

The most senior American commander on Utah was Brigadier General Theodore Roosevelt. At 57 Theodore Roosevelt was not a well man, he had trouble walking from old war wounds, and a weak heart to boot. However as the oldest soldier in the attack he was determined to lead his men, once more, into battle.

Major General Barton had tried to stop General Roosevelt from taking part in the Normandy landings due to his condition. However after Roosevelt kept pleading with him, *'Tubby'* Barton reluctantly allowed Roosevelt to go with his men. After giving him permission Barton quietly said to his colleagues that he did not expect Roosevelt to survive. How right he was! Despite a heart condition and arthritis that forced him to use a cane, Roosevelt led the assault on Utah, passing Norman's ship and landing with the first wave of troops around 6.44 am.

He would be the only general on D-Day to land by sea with the first wave of troops. Alongside Capt. Leonard T. Schroeder Jr, he leapt off his landing craft and moved onto the soft sands of Utah Beach.

With a cane in one hand and a gun in the other, shouting commands to his men, Roosevelt was the stuff of American heroes.

Troops landing on Utah.

In the star-studded film, the Longest Day, Roosevelt was played by a far too healthy and handsome Henry Fonda.

Roosevelt soon noticed something was wrong and he was informed by his men that the landing craft had drifted more than a mile south of their objective and that they were way off course. His reply was something like, "Well then boys, we'll start the war from right here!"

His action worked with complete success. With masses of artillery landing, each regiment was personally welcomed onto the beach by a cool and calm Roosevelt. He inspired everyone with his light-hearted banter and clear commands. It was as if he knew this was to be his finest hour.

For a period they were pinned down by a howitzer battery that was pounding the shoreline, but a textbook attack by men of Easy Company, led by Lt Dick Winters, knocked out the guns.

They had parachuted in as part of the 506th Parachute Infantry Regiment, E-Company 2nd Battalion. The drop had been a disaster as heavy enemy flak forced the planes to drop the men over a vast area. Many young men were killed before they even reached the ground. Dick Winters, a young Lieutenant, rounded up as many men as he could find and led the attack on the battery. Once the battery was down, men from the beach could safely move forward. The textbook enemy engagement was later immortalised by Spielberg in the film, Band of Brothers.

Nearly all of these swimming tanks made it onto Utah Beach, because, with no fear of mines, they were launched only half as far out, as at Omaha, and were able to steer into the current more effectively. Roosevelt openly stood on the beach guiding craft and men, reciting poetry and telling anecdotes about his father.

What a man! In America, love him or hate him, he is admired by all for his selfless action under fire. Roosevelt pointed almost every arriving regiment to their new objectives. He commanded the untangling of trucks and tanks struggling to get off the beach. His dedication on Utah made it one of the most successful of all the Normandy landings.

Within three hours the enemy forces, defending Utah, had surrendered and the Allied troops and supplies were moving inland.

Roosevelt shortly after the landings.

By midday, the men of the 4th Infantry had met up with some of the men from the 101st Airborne Unit. German opposition was swiftly dealt with.

By the end of the day the Americans had advanced about four miles inland and they were about one mile from the 82nd at St. Mère-Eglise, some six miles north of Carentan.

On the first full day of the landing at Utah, over 23, 470 men had landed, and 1,703 military vehicles. Casualties were around 223 men, amazingly light compared with the other beaches.

Though the war in the Cotentin Peninsula was not over, the military achievements at Utah were superb.

Because of radio silence before and during the invasion the first word of the successful landings on the French coast reached the media via the most unusual way, Gustav the carrier pigeon. Gustav was specially trained to avoid the Nazi hawks that patrolled the skies looking for carrier pigeons. He managed to get through all the enemy flak and other dangers to bring back news of the successful attack.

Gustav was released from an Allied warship and flew the 150 miles to Thorney Island with his precious message attached to his leg. For his heroic mission Gustav was awarded the Dickin Medal for gallantry. Unfortunately Gustav met a sticky end after being accidently stepped on by the cleaner mucking out his pigeon loft! The other beaches were struggling, but by the end of the first day of the invasion over 159,000 men had landed on the Normandy beaches.

As fate had it on 12 July 1944, five-weeks after the landing at Utah Beach, Theodore Roosevelt Jr died of a heart attack in France.

He is buried at the American cemetery in Normandy next to his brother, Lt. Quentin Roosevelt who had been killed in France during World War I.

The Germans kept the allies, on the British front, bottled up in a small beachhead for nearly two months, while the US forces captured their objectives on the Cherbourg Peninsular, but in the end the beachhead was broken and troops moved into central France.

The beginning of the end of the war in Europe was underway.

Unknown sailors buried at Friston Church near Eastbourne with the simple words, **Known unto God**. Casualties like these were washed up all along the coast during the War.

Chapter 19
Action Stations

On D-Day as Norman and his crew made their way back from Utah, through the rough seas and past the endless convoy of ships ferrying troops and machines to the Normandy beaches, Norman thought he saw an old friend in the sea mist. Powering past Norman at full steam was HMS *Meynell*, his old destroyer. Norman stood to attention and saluted his old comrades as they disappeared into the sea-mist toward France.

After hours of action Norman and his crew were exhausted and they needed to rest. Rather than go back to England they were ordered to keep near the action in case they were required. They tied-up next to a large destroyer that had finished unloading troops, and awaited further orders.

The crew slept in the forecastle called the *foc'sl* at the front of the ship while the officers had their quarters at the rear. They were running shifts of two-hours on two-hours off so sleep was at a premium. Food was prepared in the galley by whoever was available to cook. The officers ate in the wardroom next to their quarters at the rear or aft of ML.

The living and sleeping space for the rest of the crew was the mess deck, which had six folding bunks along each side. The mess deck took up most of the forward-hull. The officer's quarters were cramped but well designed and the top bunk would fold down to become a settee. The officer's quarters also had a small wardroom, a pantry and head. Although basic, the crew still referred to the officers as 'those lucky sods down aft.'

For a period the Germans had got their act together, and the ships were under constant attack from the few remaining German aircraft and the larger shore-based guns, situated behind the beaches. The sea was aflame with explosions and fire as great plumes of water shot skyward as the shells landed.

Suddenly one of the destroyers took a direct hit and went up in a huge explosion that broke the ship's back.

Norman saw the explosion and rushed to the bridge. There was no time to lose. "ACTION STATIONS," Norman blared. He fired up ML116 and brought his ship around and headed full-speed for the burning destroyer. He carefully brought his craft alongside the sinking vessel. This was not easy in the rough seas, and all instructions from the bridge had to be relayed via a voice tube to the helmsman, who was at the wheel in the armour-plated wheelhouse. "Port 10, port 20 slow ahead, slow, slow, amidships, stop."

As they came alongside the stricken vessel, Roy Perrot, his second-in-command, carrying all the morphine he could gather leapt aboard the burning ship.

The cold reality of war is a horrific sight. Screaming young men calling for their mothers covered in blood, burning debris everywhere and panic. Roy, a tough Welshman, stayed as long as he could and administered every drop of their morphine to the dying men to ease their pain.

Running dangerously low on fuel, Norman received orders to pull back from Normandy and make sail for Portsmouth.

Their part in the Normandy landings was finally over, his men had performed admirably and Norman felt a wave of pride come over him as he gave his orders to head for home.

They managed to dodge any more shells and made it safely back to port. Norman and his crew could breathe again for the first time in days.

Roy Perrot, the gentle Welshman who leapt aboard the stricken vessel.

Chapter 20
The Return

At Portsmouth the shore crews were amazed to see ML116 motor in, flags flying.

Norman was pretty sure that he could see money vigorously changing hands, as if bets had been placed on who would come back and who wouldn't. In fact a sweepstake had taken place and Norman's lucky streak lost several men their month's wages, which was much to Norman's delight.

Norman was filled with a sense of euphoria at his survival and so he, and his men, wasted no time getting ashore and rushing off to celebrate, not only their continued existence on planet earth but also being the first ones back from the successful landings.

First stop was the duty free shop where they blew their pay on whisky, gin, port, sherry and anything else that was available. In 1944 a bottle of whisky was six shillings and tuppence, while the gin was four shillings and tuppence, which is about 20p in today's money. They staggered away with their bottles under their arms and headed for a celebration evening aboard one of the ancient wooden hulks moored at Portsmouth.

Together they sang sea shanties and toasted their success and survival of yet another crazy mission.

Luck is everything in war. One lucky lad was my dentist's father, John Mealling. He was a Royal Engineer part of the REME, Royal Electrical and Mechanical Engineers coming ashore on Gold Beach. They were equipped with portable bridges that were to cross the Rhine.

When Mealling arrived in Normandy the worst of the fighting was over. His team slowly progressed to their allotted section of the Rhine. By March of 1945 they arrived at Remagen with their pontoon bridges, only to find out that the Germans had failed to blow it up and the Americans had already crossed.

Sergeant Alex Drabik had charged across the Ludendorff Bridge yelling to his following men before leaping into a bomb crater. He later said that he didn't stop because he knew that if he kept moving they wouldn't hit him.

The last remaining bridge across the Rhine was a tough old bridge and refused constant attempts to destroy it. By the time it did collapse the Americans had substantial forces across.

Pontoon bridges were set up so by the time the Germans had destroyed the bridge it was of little use anyway.

As the Americans moved onward John Mealling had time to spark up a relationship with a young German girl. When Mealling and his team returned to Normandy to maintain the Mulberry Harbours he kept her details. His men arrived back without as much as a scratch. Later he married the pretty German girl he met on the banks of the Rhine.

Winston Churchill and General Eisenhower shortly before crossing the Rhine. The beginning of the end of the war was now in sight.

All during hostilities Norman never wondered if they would win the war. It was something that went unquestioned. His old Kimbolton School training had stood him in good stead. One carried out one's orders and did one's duty. You were in harm's way and you either lived or died. The British Bulldog spirit kept them striving against enormous odds. But now the tide of war in Europe had changed. The combined Allied forces were slowly grinding the Germans back.

As the Pathé newsreels clicked and fluttered around in smoky cinemas all over the country, the men and women of Great Britain felt as if there was a light at the end of the tunnel.

Norman took the time, in port, to write a detailed report of his actions at Utah Beach with special mention of Roy and a commendation for his exceptional action under fire. Norman's report was later approved.

Roy was mentioned in dispatches for his outstanding bravery in the face of the enemy and awarded a bronze oak-leaf to proudly wear on the ribbon of his campaign medal.

Chapter 21

No. 17.

3rd July 1945

This is to Certify that Ty. Lieut. Harold Norman Osborne RNVR has served as Commanding Officer in H.M.M.L. 116 under my command, from the 30th day of June 1944, to the 29th day of June 1945, during which period he has conducted himself* *to my entire satisfaction a keen and capable officer who has always shown qualities of cheerfulness and loyalty.*

J.E. Page

Lieut. RNVR. { Captain H.M.S. SENIOR OFFICER 4th M.L. FLOTILLA

*Here the Captain is to insert in his own handwriting the conduct of the Officer

In June of 1945 with his task at Utah Beach over Norman was transferred to another commander for further duties as a rest after D-Day and his duties signed off by John Page, senior officer of the 4th ML flotilla.

By 29 June Norman and his crew were busy again. They carried out more short convoy and minesweeping duties along the French coast. The Germans were down but not yet beaten, so everyone kept a good lookout, especially for the fast and lethal E-Boats that appeared out of nowhere, attacked, and disappeared.

Norman's next detail was off to Granville on the French coast and then to shallow sweep the wide Gironde Estuary for mines. This would allow shipping to move further into France. After an easy patch they were now once more deep into enemy territory, and although the tide of war had turned in Europe they were back in the front line. The Gironde Estuary is a huge inlet where the mouths of two rivers, the Dordogne and the Garonne, meet in southwest France, the ancient region of Aquitaine.

It was not all bad news as Norman was to find out. He was in a convoy of four heavily armed ML's moving slowly down the estuary heading for the port of Pauillac. All the time keeping their eyes peeled for the enemy and mines.

On reaching the port of Pauillac the ships were the first of the allied forces to arrive in the area. After years of German occupation their arrival caused quite a stir. The Mayor quickly rushed to put on his best suit and meet the British sailors on the quayside. A grand reception was hurriedly laid on to welcome the liberating heroes. To help things along the cellars of Mouton Rothschild, just a stone's throw away, were raided.

Instead of being fodder for the enemy's guns, Norman and his fellow officers, of the accompanying launches found themselves as honoured guests at the first official liberation party of Pauillac.

They were the centre of attention and the enthusiastic Mayor waved his arms around energetically showering them with kisses. During the evening songs were sung and the wine flowed. Norman did his best slipping into his favourite song of *"You are my sunshine, my only sunshine'* which was met with much cheering and toasting. The celebrations went on late into the night and hidden wine stores were brought out and dusted off. Their tables were lavished with rose petals and all the food that the French could find.

The Mouton Rothschild vineyards at Pauillac were a wonderful surprise for Norman and his crew. They had been expecting German resistance instead the only pain they encountered was from their hangovers!

It was one of those special evenings that would stay with Norman for the rest of his life.

Once Norman had finished his duties at Pauillac he was ordered to the Channel Islands to sweep St Peter Port in Guernsey. It was a deep anchorage and the capital of Guernsey.

The Channel Islands had been occupied by the Germans throughout much of the war and towards the end, even though they were only a few miles from the French coast, supplies ran out. The Islanders were starving. The occupying Germans were in the same boat, no supplies meant no food for them either.

As supplies dwindled, the locals ate everything and anything, which including the cats! There were no four-legged creatures left on the islands that were not hunted. On 9 May 1945 HMS *Bulldog* arrived in St Peter Port to take the official surrender of the Germans, however, they were not the first British to take back the Islands.

A former post office worker, called Warder, had heard the surrender of the Germans on his hidden homemade crystal wireless the night before. He did not wait for the Navy to arrive. Mr Warder fearlessly marched in to the German offices based at the old post office and demanded to see the commanding officer. He informed the German officer that the war was over and that he was commandeering the building on behalf of the British Post Office!

Many Islanders knew the Germans were as happy to see the end of the war as they were. As the Germans left they had to hand over their arms, and Norman had his pick of the weapons, choosing a new officer's luger pistol that fired 9 mm rounds.

It was not going to be the only memento Norman would end up with by the time he was de-mobbed. Norman later listened to King George speak to the nation, *"Wherever you are serving in our wide, free Commonwealth of Nations, you will always feel at home. Though severed by the long sea-miles of distance you are still in the family circle."*

Chapter 22

Soon Victory in Europe was complete. VE Day had come and gone in a haze of celebrations.

As the crowds went wild in London, King George proudly waved from the balcony of Buckingham Palace. *"We want the King, we want the King,"* screamed the sea of people below. King George invited Churchill onto the balcony to riotous applause and a spontaneous rendition of Land of Hope and Glory.

Princess's Elizabeth and Margaret snuck out the back stairs of the Palace and danced in the streets with the swarms of well-wishers until 3am, then did the same the following day. Millions of people celebrated on what many say could have been the happiest day the world has ever seen.

Britain started the huge clear-up and re-build. They were in debt to the world, a debt that would take generations to repay. A few weeks later in July of 1945 a *"Khaki Election'* was held, so called as many of the men and women of the country were still in uniform. Astoundingly Winston Churchill, the most popular Prime Minister in history just a few weeks earlier, was thrown out of office losing half his seats. No one is exactly sure why this happened with his 83% rating in the polls. People said one thing and voted another. Clement Attlee, with his Labour Party, took the reins from the National Government that had struggled through the hard years of war.

Winston Churchill, though stunned, took defeat gracefully.

"The decision of the British people has been recorded in the votes counted today. I have therefore laid down the charge which was placed upon me in darker times. I regret that I have not been permitted to finish the work against Japan. For this however all plans and preparations have been made, and the results may come much quicker than we have hitherto been entitled to expect. Immense responsibilities abroad and at home fall upon the new Government, and we must all hope that they will be successful in bearing them.

It only remains for me to express to the British people, for whom I have acted in these perilous years, my profound gratitude for the unflinching, unswerving support which they have given me during my task, and for the many expressions of kindness which they have shown towards their servant."

Norman knew his Navy days were numbered as thousands of soldiers, sailors and airmen were slowly being sent home. He looked forward to being de-mobbed like the rest of the forces and getting back to civvie-street. The long hard years of Norman's war were coming to a close. But there was a final surprise in store for the young lieutenant.

As Norman waited to be de-mobbed he noticed many of his friends were being sent home before him. One day he was called to the office to receive his last orders. He brushed off his officer's uniform, polished his shoes and packed for home. At the door to the office was an old sailor leaning on the wall smoking a pipe. As Norman walked towards him, the old sailor tapped his pipe on his upturned boot and with a wry smile that only an old sea dog could give said, "Brace yer'self boy, yer in fer' a surprise." He touched the pipe to his forehead in a mock salute. Norman smiled and walked past thinking little of his words but 'surprise' was an understatement!

Chapter 23
Sumatra

To Norman the war was pretty much finished. Churchill had mentioned the Japanese in his last speech as Prime Minister and although there was fighting in the Far East that was on the other side of the world, a sort of forgotten war that few in Britain knew much about. Norman was to find out that the Far East was *"not so far'* at all!

Instead of being sent home Norman was amongst the few officers earmarked for further war duties—in Sumatra!

Orders were given for Norman to travel to Singapore and await further instructions. These orders turned out to be to sweep the bays and inlets of Islands like Sumatra with another ship and crew, and to oversee the surrender and disarmament of any Japanese that he came across.

Norman, always up for an adventure, eagerly gathered his kit and boarded a troop ship bound for Colombo. Colombo in Sri Lanka is a busy and vibrant port and had a mix of colonial buildings and ancient ruins. A few weeks later Norman found himself walking down the gang plank with his kit over his shoulder into the steamy and exotic port. He had several weeks leave in Colombo before heading for Singapore and was determined to enjoy himself.

Singapore, on the southern tip of the Malaya Peninsula, had been under Japanese control during the war and they even had their own money printed, later known as *'Banana Money'* as it became worthless. In the rainy season 14 inches of rain had been known to fall in a single day. It was to be an alien paradise to Norman. But big things were afoot in the Far East.

On 6 August 1945 President Harry S Truman, the new President of the United States who had taken the reigns after Franklin Delano Roosevelt's sudden death, announced to the world that America had harnessed the power of the universe and that we had entered the atomic age. At a highly secret location deep in the New Mexico Dessert the world's first Atomic Bomb had been built and tested.

Aboard the USS *Augusta* in the mid Atlantic, Truman gave an executive order to Paul Tibbets. He was commanding his Boeing B-

29 Super fortress named after his mother, Enola Gay. His instructions were to drop an atomic bomb, codenamed Little Boy, on Hiroshima, Japan. He carried out his orders.

On 8 August Russia declared war on Japan, and entered Manchuria.

On 9 August the bomber '*Bocks car*' flew over Kokura in Japan to drop the next weapon of mass destruction. However the city was obscured by cloud. The B-29 bomber then flew on to Nagasaki and dropped '*Fat Man*.'

The end was in sight for Japan, and Emperor Hirohito forced his fanatical commanding officers to accept the allied terms of surrender in the Potsdam Declaration.

On 15 August the Japanese finally surrendered. A day that became known as Victory over Japan or VJ Day. Mamoru Shigemitsu signed a full and unconditional surrender aboard the USS *Missouri* on 2 September 1945.

After six grueling years, the World War was almost over.

Norman found that his temporary stop before Singapore in Colombo was a dream. There were long sandy beaches to explore with warm waves rolling in from the Indian Ocean. With several weeks of leave, Norman decided that he was there and that he would enjoy them. He spent three weeks waiting for orders with other sailors visiting bars and clubs in the evening and sunbathing on the beaches during the day. It was nowhere near as bad as Norman had feared when he first had his dreaded orders back in cold, wet, Britain. In fact, it was close to paradise.

Norman spent hours whiling away the days surfing on a new invention from Hawaii called a surfboard, a heavy large forerunner of the modern board we see today. Norman and his mates would lie over the board and paddle out to sea and wait for a roller big enough to sweep them back in. They would paddle like crazy and ride the wave to shore then rush off for drinks at the beach-bar. "Better than fighting suicidal Japanese any day, eh boys?" Norman shouted to his mates as they ran across the sandy beach with their surfboards.

However the peace was broken when Norman received orders to make for Singapore, to take charge of his new Motor Launch that had arrived. His instructions were to take the craft, and crew, along with two new officers under his command, and complete basic training. Then after sea trials off the coast of Singapore, set sail for clear-up operations around Sumatra and its many islands.

Sumatra was a muddle of rivers and the Japanese had been patrolling them, many unaware that their country had already surrendered. Norman was filled with trepidation. Everyone knew the fierce reputation and blind loyalty the Japanese had for their emperor. Even though the Japanese had officially surrendered, after the horrific bombs on Hiroshima and Nagasaki, there was no telling what each individual Japanese serviceman might do, especially when confronted with the enemy that they had swore on their honour to defeat.

Norman was also to sweep many of the tiny islands between Singapore and Sumatra. The crew put their heads down and got on with their task. They roared up and down the endless muddy rivers and inlets with a show of strength, letting everyone know that the British had arrived.

Sumatra and the islands were like some long lost world from an old novel. Hot, humid and sweaty, riddled with mosquitoes and malaria. Tropical diseases were rife to those who had not grown up with them, and Norman managed to catch one which stayed with him for life, bubbling up on his head now and again. However the tropical rainforest was also a joy to behold for a young sailor from England.

The backbone of Sumatra is lined with active volcanoes, and wild animal were everywhere. Orangutans, tigers, clouded leopards, sun bears, weird stripped rabbits, elephants and rhinoceros. Along with all these exotic creatures were hundreds of different species of birds in every colour, shape and size. On his journeys Norman became more like Darwin than a naval officer, transfixed by the beauty of this untouched world.

Chapter 24
Surrender!

All this came home to cold reality when Norman received orders that a Japanese lightship, off one of the hundreds of prominent rocky peninsulas, had not surrendered! Plans were drawn up for Norman to take the lightship and replace its Japanese crew with Indonesians, who would be trained to keep its light shining.

Once again, as all his mates back home were at work on civvie street, Norman was in the thick of it. Yet another dangerous mission was underway. He had a stark choice. He could go in with guns blazing, mount a surprise attack at night or take the bull by the horns and meet the Japanese head on. Norman decided the latter.

With a full crew and the trained Indonesians on board, Norman had his men take up positions on all the artillery. In plain daylight with full flags flying, and all hands on deck, they moved slowly toward the Japanese light ship, making no sudden movements, and keeping their weapons down. To Norman's relief the Japanese did not open fire. Slowly Norman gave orders for his ship to pull alongside the Japanese vessel. Now was the point of no return.

Norman boarded the waiting ship with one of his officers and a translator. If anything went wrong now all hell would break loose. All the men were ready. One itchy trigger-finger would spell a disastrous end for Norman's years of war.

The Japanese officers came forward toward Norman, and the commanding officer placed his hand on his samurai sword. Norman's heart was in his mouth, his hand resting on his holstered German luger. The Japanese officer bowed, and with both hands unclipped his sword and handed it horizontally to Norman. Norman took his sword and bowed his head in return. The crew on both sides started to breathe again. Norman's second in command relieved the other officer of his weapons and the crew stood down.

Norman's lucky streak was still with him.

The transfer of crews took place and soon Norman and his crew were taking the Japanese sailors back to Singapore, for their homeward passage. The famous Raffles Hotel called *'Light of the*

South', by the Japanese, was used as a transit camp for prisoners of war.

To Norman's credit during the entire war he never lost a man under his command. Norman gave his orders with friendly and firm confidence and would rather have a drink and a song with his men than throw shouts at them. His methods had gone a long way to his many crews surviving the war in one piece, and what he learnt in handling young adults was to have long-reaching effect on his later life.

Norman's war was finally coming to an end. All the last Japanese were rounded up and sent home, and the British sailors too. And so, still clutching a samurai sword, Norman hopped aboard a troop ship bound for Colombo and home.

Resting in Colombo, Norman and a few of his mates got itchy feet and decided to go and see the famous tea plantations. They took local buses and walked for hours. They passed through small villages with corrugated iron or leaf roofs slowly winding up into the hills of Ceylon, now Sri Lanka. They stopped for a bite to eat, and carried on through forests of sweetly scented cinnamon trees into the highlands, constantly enthralled by the scenery. By late evening they were completely lost. However in the fading light they spotted the rising patio-layered fields of a tea plantation. At the top they saw a light on in a house and decided to ask for help.

"How in God's name did you end up here boys?" Said the man holding a glass of whisky in one hand and a rifle slung under the other. "You're bloody lucky to find me I'm the only white man for 20 miles! If the separatists had got you, you'd never been heard of again! Ever heard of the Tamil Hill People?" The exhausted lads shook their heads. "No—, well you will boys, you mark my words, they are as fierce as their tigers and they love to hold the odd European for ransom."

Mr. Purn was a British Ex-Pat running the tea plantation, and was delighted to see some boys from the old country. He took them in, fed them supper, got them drunk and sang songs with them till they passed out. The next day, after almost sobering up and finally sampling the tea they had come so far to taste, he kindly took them the long drive back to their naval base. He drove like a maniac, swerving and swearing down the lethal winding roads back towards Colombo.

They all climbed out of the car in Colombo with sweat dripping off them, and shaking. Purn spun the car round, hooted and disappeared in a cloud of dust. "Bleedin Nora that was the worst drivin' I ever did see," said one of Norman's mates as they headed for the nearest bar to recover.

After a few weeks in Colombo, Norman gained passage aboard a troop ship and made the long homeward journey back to Britain. On route Norman realised that after all his years at sea this would be his last trip as a naval officer. Upon hearing about this the captain called him to the bridge, and as a special favour allowed Norman to take the Late Watch.

It was to be his last command as an officer in the British Navy.

Chapter 25
Norman's war comes to an end, At Last!

At Norman's demobilization there was no old sailor waiting with a warning. This time his war was finally over. In February of 1946 Norman was awarded a £50 gratuity, to help kick-start his life in civvie-street. He was also given a suit. Norman said that there were three different qualities of suits being handed out. The top brass had tailor-made pure wool, the officers, Worsted cloth, and the rest of the men shoddy cloth, a mixture of pulverized off-cuts that was reformed into material, and sewn into suits and coats.

For the first time in six years, on a bitterly cold February morning, Norman walked out of the naval base a free man. He carried with him just about everything he owned in the world, including his war souvenirs. First stop was home to see Dad and make sure his old Hetchins bicycle was still in one piece.

The war was over and the men who had risked their lives almost on a daily basis went back to work. The men of the Coastal Forces who had crossed each other's paths in war now looked for other roads to follow. Harold Fisch, commanding officer on board HMS *Meynell* went to Oxford to teach English Literature. Lennox-Boyd went into politics and later became embroiled in the Mau Mau uprisings in Kenya. Lt. Cdr Peter Scott, son of the famous Scott of the Antarctic, who had like Norman, also served in the North Atlantic before moving to the coastal forces, wrote down his war memories. Among his many achievements in later life he helped found the world famous Wildlife and Wetlands Trust.

Norman moved back in with his Dad for a while and received his de-mob papers and medals. Sixty five years later, in 2011, an extra medal arrived for his part in the Far East.

In the evenings, after supper, they would often sit together and listen to a new radio show called Dick Barton Special Agent. The show was so popular that it ran for hundreds of episodes. Dick, with his best friends, Snowy White and Jock Anderson would find themselves in all sorts of scrapes, and 15 million followers would be leaning towards their sets listening to how the group would manage to escape from their weekly predicament. In post-war Britain Dick

Barton, the mythical ex-commando, became the nation's favourite sleuth.

Norman pondered on what to do with his gratuity money before it was all wasted. He decided to commission a modern Hetchings bicycle, well 1946 modern anyway. After eight weeks the bike arrived. The new Hetchins was sparkling and fast but Norman never warmed to it like his old Hetchins, bought from the Morris Brothers all those years before. "I think my bum had taken the same shape as the old saddle and never warmed to the new one." Norman said.

Norman's old job at Zurich Insurance was held open for him and soon he found new lodgings in North London. Each day he would make his way through the bomb-blitzed city back to his old job. Climbing over rubble and making constant detours around closed streets he would eventually weave his way to work. He quickly bonded back with his workmates, many of them who had also fought in the war.

His new lodgings were run by a kind old landlady, and one day Norman decided to treat the old dear to a drink at the pub down the road. It was no secret that during the war years Norman had given up his tea-total Navy allowance when he became an officer, and enjoyed many a good tipple with his men. After a dangerous convoy, as the commanding officer on better pay than his men, he often bought the first round.

Rum rations were a daily occurrence on board ship. Rum was known as '*Grog*' or '*Nelson's Blood*' and at midday the bosun would blow his whistle or 'pipe-up' shouting out, "*Up spirits.*" The men would take their rum ration and shout, "*Stand fast for the Holy Ghost,*" before swigging down the rum and getting back to work. It was one of the many traditions of the Royal Navy. If you decided not to drink you could take the official, TTA, *Tea-Total Allowance*, of three-pence-a-day. There were three alcohol abbreviations, G, T, and U. U was underage when the sailor was too young to drink. G was *Grog Allowance,* which meant a daily swig of booze and T was *Temperance Allowance*, three-pence extra pay for not drinking at all.

With the pressures of war Norman had soon given up his *Temperance Allowance* and became a G or '*Grog*' rating for alcohol and enjoyed his daily tot-of-rum. He was also a regular at many pubs along the coast like the Rising Sun, his local in Ramsgate, or the Woolpack in Chilham, Kent, where Lennox-Boyd, his old flotilla commander, once took over the entire pub for his farewell bash. However he was unknown at this new pub. Although Norman had seen service in some of the most hostile waters and countries in the world, he was still a short and youthful looking lad.

At the new pub, with his landlady comfortable seated, he went to the bar to order his drinks. There was a gruff look from the barman who said to him that he had to be 16 to drink and told him to leave. "Okay sonny boy be 'orf with ya' and sharpish, come back in a few years when you have to shave!"

Embarrassed, Norman was taken aback. However he was quickly aided by his lovely landlady, who leapt up and gave the barman an ear-bashing, explaining how Norman had fought for his country so that people like him could still have a job. A red-faced barman apologized and free drinks duly arrived.

Back at Zurich Insurance, filling out motor claims was just not the same for Norman. He had seen a whole new world of excitement, and sifting through insurance papers was no fun now. After a few months back at the old firm Norman made the decision to leave.

Chapter 26
Oxford

Norman decided that he would like to take a degree course and become a teacher.

He applied for a course at one of the finest universities in the world, Oxford. With some strong recommendations from fellow officers, and character references from his old Kimbolton School, Norman was lucky enough to be accepted. Even his old headmaster, the redoubtable William Ingram, wrote to Oxford a few perfect words, *"His sterling character and pleasing personality will render him an invaluable asset."*

University College Oxford

Oxford University, the oldest English speaking university in the world, was founded centuries before Norman stepped inside its hallowed halls. At present Oxford University is split up into 36 colleges.

Each college has sports teams, such as Exeter College, where the great actor Richard Burton had been, or Magdalene pronounced 'Maudlin' where Robert Hardy was studying before becoming the well-loved actor in All Creatures Great and Small. From the cream of the individual colleges, single teams were picked to represent Oxford University as a whole. Playing in the first team of your college won you College Colours. Rowing practice for the famous Oxford-Cambridge boat race would take place on local rivers, like the ancient River Isis that flowed through Oxford down to London to join the Thames.

Norman in the second row, and his Oxford friends at a football match sponsored by Jeyes Fluid.

Sport and competition is, like the river, the lifeblood that runs through Oxford joining all its colleges. When Norman enrolled for his degree course at the 13th century Univ, or University College, smack in the centre of Oxford, Roger Bannister was running his socks off around the track. No one knew that a few years later he would become the fastest man alive. Tony Benn the labour politician was just finishing the studies that he had started before the war, along with many other famous people. Norman was soon involved in cricket, football, boxing and squash and became club secretary, organizing many of the events.

Because of the war and Norman's role in it for six years of his life, he was older than many of his fellow students, and he became a natural organizer and team leader. Norman took the opportunity to get Kimbolton School to play at Oxford and vice-a-versa, introducing the Dean at Oxford to the Kimbolton Headmaster.

Before long Norman was studying hard and playing even harder. He attacked sports with energy and zeal. Whether it was squash, football or boxing, he loved it all. Norman was lucky that his teachers failed to find out that, amongst many of Oxford's strange events that had taken place while he was studying there, that it was him that was responsible for the renting of the medieval highway coach that caused chaos along the Oxford roads, while taking his mates to cricket at Cumnor!

On the way back, drunk and covered in cows muck from playing cricket on a local farmer's field they lost control of the coach and had to steer it into a ditch to save from running amuck in Oxford.

The coach that the group later lost control of, coming back from their Cumnor cricket match. Norman can just be seen in the middle laughing. He was not laughing so much when the coach was out of control.

Norman joined the Utopers which was a beer drinking society thinly disguised as a sporting club and some of their sports fixtures were more of a booze-up than a match. "We were quite good at sport, but unbeatable at drinking." Norman proudly winked when retelling his tales to me.

In the main dining hall you had to be careful of what you said and how you acted, for there was the penalty of the Sconce!

If the house president in charge of the common room decided that you had done or said something that needed punishing, he would administer the Sconce. Beer was brought up from the ancient cellars beneath the common room and the challenge started. A huge silver tankard was filled with two-and-a-half pints of beer. To tumultuous cheering and goading from the whole room you had to drink the complete tankard—without throwing up—within one minute! This was a deed that few accomplished. However if you did succeed then it became the turn of the president to drink the tankard. If he managed all the beer, the guilty student then had to repeat his procedure until one failed or passed out.

Norman told me that these carefree days were some of the happiest of his life.

However at the end of his first term Norman failed some of his exams miserably. A note was included with his term results by his tutor, *"Mr. Albone seems to have forgotten all the history he had learnt at school."* A term later, after some hard studying, Norman passed his exams with distinction. This time his tutors note was more positive. *"Mr. Albone has surprised the world."*

Oxford was in its own world, and, as the country prepared for the London Olympics in 1948, Oxford had different plans.

For Oxford Universities 700 year celebrations a great Masque was to be held. A masque was from medieval times, where a huge pageant of entertainment was put on including dancing, singing and acting.

The Oxford Masque was to coincide with Princess Elizabeth receiving an honorary doctorate in the spring of 1948. And so Oxford prepared to resurrect the ancient pageant.

Part of the Oxford Masque held in 1948

A year previously the Princess had married her dream man, the imposing Lieutenant Phillip Mountbatten. The handsome Greek-born prince had fought throughout the war in the Royal Navy even though two of his brother-in-laws had fought for Germany. Later in the war Phillip had served as an instructor at Norman's first training camp, *Royal Arthur*, in Skegness.

Rationing was still in force in England in 1948 and there was little surplus money at Oxford to celebrate, however the dawning of a new age needed something special. The Masque was really a political satire comparing the doom and gloom of the Conservatives attitudes with the positive new outlook of the Labour Party. Something that if Winston Churchill had grasped sooner would have kept him in power after the war.

It was a complex affair that few understood. Student-actors were playing parts like Venus, Neptune, Hope, Tyranny and Fear. They were performing bizarre pieces in a very peculiar spectacle, in front of a bemused Princess.

Robert Hardy, with his back to us, fights another student.

Princess Elizabeth's walk to the event was timed to the second. All along her route from the High Street, over Magdalen Bridge and into the University was brightened with bunting and flags. The Dons were wearing black, scarlet and pink gowns. The whole place was crammed with spectators staring from every space and every window. As the Princess entered University College, to riotous applause, the Royal Standard broke out on the masthead above the buildings. Few knew that, as the Princess glided past, she was already pregnant with her first child.

Princess Elizabeth is met by the University College Master.

The day's events unfolded with a blinding rapidity of confusion, action and colour, with silk, velvet and chiffon everywhere. It was a medieval masterpiece brought back to life after centuries asleep.

Robert Hardy had a sword fight against the flamboyant student playing Knowledge, and hundreds of doves were simultaneously released in the College quadrangle courtyard.

The Master's wife next to Elizabeth. No one knew she was pregnant.

All-in-all a completely confusing and memorable event in which the Princess bloomed. Norman said that it was probably more for the intellectuals but there was enough humour, colour and action to keep everyone riveted. Even the BBC turned up to film it, though what the viewers made of it all on their tiny black-and-white televisions at home must have been a mystery.

Later in the summer the Olympic Games got underway in London. King George VI spoke impressively in front of 80,000 spectators in his opening speech. The first games since the 1936 Berlin Games got started without Germany or Japan, both were banned.

The games were a stern affair, no new buildings were erected, and all the competitors were housed in existing homes and food rationing applied to competitors as well as the public. The *'Flying Housewife'* Fanny Blankers-Koen from Holland won four gold medals and set six Olympic records and Bob Mathias, the young American, at just 17, became the youngest athlete to ever win a gold medal in the decathlon. The Russians and Americans swept the medal board and Britain, with just three gold's, two in rowing and one in sailing, went back to work.

Chapter 27

During his time at Oxford, Norman would regularly return to see his dad at his shop in St Neots. Often he would wander up the road to enjoy the Picture Palace. In 1948 the epic western Red River was just out with John Wayne drawing in the crowds. In the same year Laurence Olivier directed and starred in Shakespeare's masterpiece, Hamlet.

St Neots High Street was Norman's playground as a kid. He would often rush up the pot-holed road and climb the fence to watch the cattle being sold at the cattle market. Now the town was bustling with cars, buses, motorcycles and it even had electric street lighting. The shops that he used to run to each week with his mum's scribbled out shopping list had all changed hands. The market stalls where fresh cakes and farmers pies came out on display each week had been cleared away to make room for new buildings. However the heart of the town was still there and Norman loved it.

A chance meeting with an old school friend outside the Picture Palace one weekend led to another adventure. Norman had always fancied an epic bike ride, and he had planned a great route up through the Lake District to West Scotland and through the Highlands, covering hundreds of miles.

John Annett, an old Kimbolton friend, was also a keen cyclist and just the lad to join Norman on his ambitious trip. They serviced and polished their bikes, jammed all they could into their rucksacks and set off, up the Great North Road toward the Highlands of Scotland.

Two weeks cycling around the muddy roads of 1940's Scotland, staying in basic youth hostels, left both men yearning for a warm comfy bed. On the way back down from York, Norman popped in on Gwen, his old flame from Newhaven during the war. She was now happily married and living in Oakham in Rutland, and though surprised to see Norman turn up she was delighted to see his same old cheeky smile. Over afternoon tea they reminisced on the war days. Later Norman met back up with John and headed for home.

Norman and John cycled hard heading south, and the night before arriving back at St Neots they used their last money to book in to a proper hotel with baths! Two weeks of hard cycling, youth hostels and camping had left the pair desperate for a soak in a warm tub!

Norman Passed out of Oxford in 1949 with his degree. However what meant most to him was not his qualifications, not even his College Colours as football captain and nippy left winger. It was not the annual competition with Trinity Hall Cambridge that meant the most, but in the end it was the winning of the prize for the best all round student at the College. This was a great honour as it showed that he was liked by staff and pupils, and this meant more than words could ever express.

What to do next was the question? The post-grad year flew past and after applying for a couple of teaching posts, an old Navy pal told Norman about a fantastic opportunity in Africa.

He recommended Norman for a teaching post in Kenya. Lennox-Boyd had served alongside Norman on his own ML113 and they had shared many-a-perilous journey on the High Seas and through E-Boat Alley off Lowestoft. Later Lennox-Boyd's career would suffer with the infamous Mau Mau rebellion in Kenya.

Norman's teaching appointment was approved with the help of some good references from old teachers like David Cox whose brother, Sir Christopher Cox, just happened to be at the Colonial Office and was happy to oblige. For Norman's next chapter in his life he was off to Africa.

Chapter 28
Africa

In 1951 Norman found himself dressed in khaki shorts staring down the Great Rift Valley in all its rugged glory. Another adventure had begun for our old Kimbolton boy.

The word Kenya then pronounced 'keeenya' comes from the look of the snow-capped peak of the magnificent Mount Kenya, which, to local tribesman looks like the white feathers of the male ostrich. The name Kenya translates into English as '*The place with ostriches*'.

Kenya is a varied land of plenty that lies across the equator and ranges from scenic highlands and mountains, to deserts and rolling grasslands. There are flat plains and bush filled with wild game, forests and warm tropical beaches. Kenya has it all.

Compared to Britain, Kenya had hardly been touched by the war. A bit of trouble from the Italians early on had left no mark, nor had the internment camps. By the time Norman arrived the bustling multicultural country was as vibrant as it had ever been. A melting pot of over 40 different ethnic groups. The tribes and religions all lived together in the country bordered by Uganda to the west, Tanzania and Somalia to the east and to the north by Sudan and Ethiopia.

Kenya also has an idyllic coastline straight out of a holiday brochure, miles of soft white sand lapped by the Indian, or Kenyan Ocean, where turtles swim and struggle awkwardly ashore to lay their eggs on special moonlit nights. The shoreline is laced with leaning cashew-nut trees and palm trees and dotted with small fishing villages drying their nets in the sun. Off-shore, lay archipelagoes and coral reefs which are home to countless numbers of marine life.

Kenya was a brave new world and a real challenge for Norman. He headed for the capital, Nairobi, where he studied briefly under the great teacher Carey Francis who was responsible for perfecting the Kenyan Alliance High School. At the school the cream of the Kenyan youth were taught. They were to form the next independent state of Kenya, free from British rule.

Norman had brought his Channel Islands luger with him, just in case. Though decommissioned, it might prove a deterrent to any trouble he would come across in the wilds of Africa. His forces training had stayed with him and the old saying, "*It is better to have a gun and not need it, than to need a gun and not have it,*" still held true. As it turned out Kenya was a pleasure and Norman was even to meet his future wife there.

As an education officer, employed by the Kenyan Government, Norman was responsible for finding some of the future generation of young people that would be capable of running the country. Surprisingly there were several old Oxford lads in Kenya and Norman would meet up with them on a regular basis. Norman learnt to drive and drove several other people's cars always being careful to make the correct hand signs as there were no car indicators in those days.

In the February of 1952, Princess Elizabeth and Prince Phillip were staying at Treetops at the Abedare Nation Park in Kenya, when news was brought to them that her father, King George, had died.

Elizabeth was well aware that her father was gravely ill. He had already undergone major operations such as having his left lung removed, and by November of 1951 he was too weak to read the King's Speech for the opening of Parliament. All his years of stress and smoking, tireless work and duty had caught up with him. Although he could not do the Parliament speech he managed to record his Christmas Speech to the nation in small sections, over a few weeks, and had it edited together just in time for Christmas.

On 31 January, 1952, although on death's door, and against fierce objections from doctors and staff, he managed get to the airport to see Elizabeth off on her tour. He knew in his heart that he would never see his beloved daughter again. It was his final farewell to his beautiful girl. He stayed on the cold tarmac watching the plane for ages until it finally disappeared from view, wiping away a tear that he said was from the bitter wind. No one can imagine the pain he felt as he saw Elizabeth leaving for the last time.

A few days later on 6 February, 1952 King George, the last Emperor of India, the last King of Ireland, and the first head of the new Commonwealth, died in his sleep from a blood clot to the heart. He had died in the same place that he was born, at Sandringham. He was just 56.

While an empire mourned and the dead King lay in state, Elizabeth rushed back from Treetops to Britain. Norman put his best foot forward and got down to work in Kenya finding the freedom of the wild country a breath of fresh air. The England he had left was still climbing out of recession, just the opposite to the wide open expanse of Africa.

Norman managed to get hold of his first car, an old Morris Oxford. It was a tough old banger, perfect for the lumpy, dusty roads of Africa. One night after an evening with friends Norman, a little worse for wear and a few drinks '*down the hatch*', as he would say, was bombing back to his digs at the headmaster's house when he over steered on a bend. Norman was desperately fighting with the wheel and thinking maybe drinking and driving wasn't such a good idea, even if he was in the middle of nowhere, when the car suddenly lurched from side to side and slewed into a ditch. The car rolled over onto its roof then crashed back on to its wheels and ground to a halt!

Norman clambered out of the car and shook his head. He looked around as the dust settled into the dark African night. There was nothing, no noise, no one to see what had happened just Norman and his car. He looked at the car, and, back on its wheels it hardly showed any signs of the calamity that had just occurred. Norman scratched his head, climbed back in, and pulled the starting lever. The Oxford fired up! He negotiated the car back onto the road and drove it home—at a much slower pace. He did not have a scratch on him!

After teaching at the Alliance High School, next stop was a post at Kakamega School which just happened to have a nice nine-hole golf course along with a squash court. The Kakamega Golf Club bar was the central meeting point for many of the officers, district, agricultural, medical or, like Norman, educational officers as well as several old Oxford lads. At Christmas the Kakamega Golf Club put on a pantomime but because Norman had only just arrived, the only position left unfilled was the part of the fairy! Norman played his part very seriously, dancing on as the Christmas Fairy to much applause in the smoke filled club.

Often meals would be held at the different officer's houses. Norman hooked up with a local doctor and they formed a firm friendship, often playing squash or just meeting for drinks at the golf club. During emergencies they would jump into Norman's car and race to the afro-native hospital in Kitui to carry out an emergency operations. On several occasions, much to Norman's dislike, he ended up assisting with the operations.

A term at Kikuyu School polished off Norman's teaching skills and he was on the move again. Norman started to find out all the best places to be, like the golf club at Kakamega which not only had golf but indoor squash courts, or Rosteman's Gold Mine where they had a good bar and facilities for tennis and snooker.

The food in Kenya was as varied as the people and there was plenty of everything although sometimes he was not quite sure of what he was eating! For example the Maasai ate simple foods supplied by their herds of goats and cattle. They never touched wild food or fish. This was unlike the tribes living on the edge of Lake Victoria, whose stable diet was their daily catch of fish mixed with rice, any extra fish was sold at the market or roadside. The Kikuyu grew corn, beans, potatoes and greens which they mashed all together to make Irio. They would roll the Irio into balls and dip them into meat stews.

Local Maasai herdsmen.

The basic staple foods were maize, potatoes, meat and beans with a variety of fruits, some unknown to Norman, but tasty all the same. *Ugali* was a mix of maize and meat and *sukuma* reminded Norman of cabbage back home. *Nyama Choma* was roasted meats and along the dirt roads men would roast corn for passers by, with snacks like *Mandaazi* which tasted like a doughnut of deep fried sweet dough. Women would sit in small brightly coloured groups chatting and peeling fruits and vegetables for sale. Sometimes they would spontaneously break out into laughter or songs as they worked. One favourite roadside treat was a pancake wrapped around a fried egg and minced meat.

Of course Kenya was also famous for its coffee and tea or '*chai*' plantations and to this day Norman has never had a better cup of tea than in Kenya.

One day Norman had a chance meeting at a dinner with a young English woman named Doris Eagle, who was in Kenya training teachers around Nairobi. As a teacher Doris had reserved occupation status during the war and she moved on to training teachers in Kenya. The meeting between Norman and Doris would change both of their lives. Though Doris was slightly older they were instantly attracted, and in that far off land with the hot African wind blowing, Norman and Doris fell in love. It was a love that was to last a lifetime.

Doris Eagle

Things got a bit tricky with the Mau Mau uprisings but the couple were moved to semi-detached bungalows next to each other at Embu. The Mau Mau were African Nationalists whose aim was to remove British rule from Kenya, by any means. Almost at the same time that Norman had arrived in Kenya, rumours started to appear in the capital about a group of fanatics who had taken an oath to kill any white man in Africa.

In 1952 the Mau Mau had declared open rebellion against white rule. To combat the fanatics, who slaughtered white people and their own alike, Governor General, Sir Evelyn Baring, imposed the death penalty on any Mau Mau caught trying to carry out his oath.

It all came to a head in 1954 when the Kenyan Government, with the help of British forces, rounded up over 40,000 Kikuyu tribesmen. In protest Treetops, the hotel where Princess Elizabeth had stayed was burnt to the ground. It was a dark time in British colonial history with many atrocities on both sides. Concessions from all feuding parties and the emerging independence of Kenya saw things settle down, and the state of emergency came to an end in 1959.

Once again as the Mau Mau terrorised parts of Kenya with their dreaded panga, a machete for shrub and forest clearing, with which they killed animals and humans alike, Norman was lucky and carried on his teaching, escaping without so much as a scratch. There is no doubt that the Mau Mau would have been very aware of Norman, a white man, moving around rural parts of Kenya. But Norman's main aim was towards helping the Kenyan people to self rule which was also the Mau Mau's aim. This probably kept him safe.

Chapter 29
Norman gets married

While all this was going on Norman and Doris were busy beating the other teachers at tennis, learning about Africa, keeping away from killer snakes, like the puff adder, and teaching the young men and women in various schools who would one day take over the country.

On New Year's Eve 1955, surrounded by local friends, Norman dressed in a smart dark double-breasted tailor-made Narobi suit and Doris Henrietta Eagle, with flowers in her hair and a bouquet of roses, carnations and freesias, walked up the aisle in a small rural church in Machakos.

After their wedding they had a simple reception with their friends in the garden of their local school.

Norman and Doris on their wedding day in Machakos, December 1955.

On their honeymoon they travelled to all the beautiful places of Kenya and Uganda that they did not have time to see while they were busy working.

They stayed at the Kitale Club in the highlands near Nairobi, and sailed up the Nile in a small craft watching Nile crocodiles and hippos bask in the heat of the African sun. Norman was in his element back on water. They travelled, like explorers, through Queen Elizabeth Game Park and were covered in spray from

Murchison Falls known by the locals as Kabalega Falls. Murchison Falls are not as wide as Victoria Falls (Mosi-oa-Tunya, the smoke that thunders), but at Murchison Falls the water from Lake Victoria drops over 400 feet, creating rainbows in the sun with dramatic cascades of water as it drops towards Lake Kyoga and Lake Albert.

Wild elephants and a water hole at the Queen Elizabeth Game Park.

Nowhere they stayed had double beds! So each night they would push their two single beds together. At one of the new resorts they bumped into an old Navy colleague who had been at Newhaven with Norman, Peter Scott. Peter was painting the wildlife and was deeply involved in its conservation. Later he would be influential in setting up the World Wildlife Fund. "Well knock me down with a feather, Norman Albone in the middle of Africa! We need a drink to celebrate. What on earth are you doing here?"

Norman introduced his new wife to Peter over drinks. "You won't find a double bed in Kenya mate they don't have them." Peter told the couple over dinner. "You'll have to have one made or stick two singles together when you get back home."

By the time the honeymoon was over Norman and Doris had seen the real Africa in all its rugged beauty. They had seen everything from the snow capped peek of Mount Kilimanjaro to the Kenyan plains bursting with wild game. The newlyweds, refreshed and eager to continue their teaching careers, returned to teacher training school at Maseno.

They were in for a surprise. Strangely, the law of the time in Kenya stated that if you married while in government service your wife had to give up her work. And so Doris had no choice but to become a housewife. In truth she did help Norman most of the time with his work. Norman studied hard and in the evenings learnt Swahili from the local tribesmen. This had several benefits, one being a pay rise.

In 1956 news came that Princess Margaret was making a visit to Kenya visiting schools and businesses. The hypnotic beauty not only entranced celebrities of the day like Noel Coward and Frank Sinatra but a nation as well. Her tour caused great speculation and gossip, for a rumour had spread that Princess

Margaret may have had an illegitimate child who was brought up in Kenya, supposedly hushed up by the Palace in London. It was only speculation but it kept many tongues wagging over dinner party drinks in Kenya.

The story was that a young lad called Robert Brown was the child of Princess Margaret. A cover story was allegedly made that the fake mother was a model working for the Queen's dressmaker, Hardy Amis. Of course it was all speculation fuelled by no more that gossip. The rumours increased, when she was spotted in Kenya with a white child in her car.

Years later after the Princess's death, to squash the continuing rumours, mainly by a grown up Robert Brown himself, who said he was 12th in line for the throne, Prince Charles gave a DNA sample. It showed that Brown's blood was not related to his.

Norman and Doris rushed off to see the beautiful young Princess, still in her prime before she succumbed, like her father to smoking and drinking.

Princess Margaret was radiant while in Kenya

At Machakos a large central auditorium was built for the royal visit. Local tribes came and put on a dazzling display dressed in ostrich feathers, swirling around with their spears and shields. The noise and colour was amazing. As all the action was going on, a large black open-backed limousine slowly pulled up and several dignitaries emerged, then out stepped Princess Margaret.

She was breathtaking and she stunned the crowds smiling, chatting and waving. Eventually after a local tour and a speech she disappeared back into her huge black limo and rolled off down the old dirt track.

The Princess at Machakos in 1956

What a day. Norman and Doris returned exhausted but so excited they could not sleep. They stayed up half the night chatting about the Princess, what she wore and what she had said.

After various posts Norman was later rewarded with his own school. From his new school Norman would travel into the bush to the local villages to find potential pupils to teach. Bright students were sought out, and the ones that were too far from home could board at the school.

Norman had become headmaster at Kitui. Its full name was The Government African School of Kitui, Kenya. Norman soon simplified it to Kitui School. Kitui was a *'Boma'* or small township. In Kitui, electricity had yet to conquer and oil lamps lit the classes after dark, with large moths and other insects fluttering around them.

Norman got stuck into teaching English and mathematics amongst a whole raft of other subjects. In the evenings Norman and Doris would sit on the porch and watch the African sun go down. Doris would sew up clothes on her hand sewing machine and they would keep up with news from home by listening to the World Service, when the battery allowed. No television, just their own little piece of Africa.

Norman often took bible classes under the African sky entrancing
the local children with ancient bible stories of good and evil.

Norman and his staff taught everything at Kitui that was needed
to bring out the very best in his students. He loved his work and got
stuck in, like always, with vigour. He organized electricity
generators much to the governor's disgust, and brighter gas lamps
for the school. He also brought with him his love for sport and
regularly taught the lads how to box, and played football with the
bare-footed pupils. Norman always had to be careful as he would
wear his old Oxford rubber boots, with a full set of studs!

The girl's school encouraged sports of all kinds and American basketball was their favourite.

Although not officially employed, Doris did help at the school. The pupils loved her music classes, especially the harmonium lessons. Children from around the village would sit and listen to her play, and the sounds of the choir would drift over the African grasslands.

Now, this was not your normal school, for example one day an enormous rock python came slithering into the school looking for an easy meal. Norman's half-wild dog, a wire-haired terrier named Jock, went ballistic. Rock pythons can grow to over 20 feet and devour full-size game like gazelle or impala, they are not to be sneered at.

As pandemonium broke out with screaming pupils running everywhere, local farmers rushed to the rescue and dispatched it with a machete.

That was not the end of the story. After proudly displaying the beast to all onlookers Norman ran and got his camera for pictures. Then they took the snake away. A few weeks later they returned with beautiful snakeskin handbags for Doris and the other females at the school.

Part of the python that terrorised the school and later became handbags!

Jock, who the locals had renamed '*Mwindaji*', Swahili for hunter, eventually disappeared into the bush, preferring trying to kill the wild life rather than stay with his home comforts.

Norman and Doris did well with the pupils and the school went from strength to strength, many students leaving and applying for government jobs. In May of 1957 Doris called Norman into their small pretty bungalow lined with rose bushes, and broke some wonderful news. She was expecting their first child.

On one of Norman's trips home he just managed to slip through the Suez Canal which had turned into a hotbed of Arabic dissent against the West. The Egyptian President, Gamal Nasser, was using the Canal as a pawn in a political struggle for power. Once again Lucky Norman made it home with a smile.

In November of 1957 Christopher was born and four years later in 1961, just as the Cold War worsened in Europe and the Berlin Wall began splitting Berlin in half, their second son Jeremy came into the world.

When Archbishop Beecher heard that Norman and Doris had another child he made a special journey down to Kitui to personally attend the christening of Jeremy.

It was a huge honour for Norman and Doris to have such an imposing figurehead at their tiny church service. To many of the local tribesmen the bishop was almost a god and he was treated like some sort of deity.

Jeremy's christening.

The years flew by and the school developed, they even had a proper football pitch mowed by a local farmer and his ox. A small farm grew on the edge of the school grounds so that the pupils could have fresh vegetables and local fruit like mangoes, Kenyan long bananas and pineapples. The pineapples grew low to the ground like little land mines of exploding spikes.

The school at Kitui had six dormitories for the pupils and seemed quite modern by the standards of the day, but with Nairobi 120 hard miles away shopping for anything but '*the basics*' needed a three-day trip.

The world for Norman and Doris revolved around their little township as they set about their daily chores.

Kitui was an intermediate school and Norman taught there from 1956 until 1961, developing the school into a secondary school. And, even after he finished at the school, being promoted to District Educational Officer in Nairobi, he kept an eye on the school right up until he left Africa.

As Educational Officer in Nairobi, Norman's responsibilities changed once again. He was now overseeing schools, a bit like OFSTED is today. He would travel around Kenya visiting schools and making sure everything was in order. His inspections were low-key affairs making sure each school was running at its best. Norman's directness, willingness to engage with other people, his ability to listen to their needs and his courteous manner won him many friends in Kenya.

The old colonial power of the British Empire was fading fast and by the early 1960's many of her jewels were falling like dominoes. Kenya became independent on 12 December 1963. By this time the Kenyan Educational Office had replaced Norman's job with a naturalized Kenyan.

His dismissal letter was polite and brief. Norman had known for a long time that his position in Kenya was a temporary, but it was a sad day all the same. Once he had taught the men who would become the teachers his job no longer existed.

The last family picnic in Africa before setting sail for home

Norman was looking forward, and schooling for his own boys back in England was his prime motivation. He would get his family home and start afresh.

In the summer of 1963, armed with an outstanding reference from the archbishop of East Africa, Norman and his family stood on the bustling docks at Mombasa. They loaded all their belongings on board ship and set sail. They stopped at Durban, then Cape Town, with a quick trip up Table Mountain and then homeward bound via the Canary Islands, Madeira and finally to Southampton, a port Norman knew well from his war years.

Chapter 30
Home Again

Norman arrived home to his beloved Britain in the autumn of 1963. He was back in the country that he had served all those years earlier.

After 44 wandering years Norman was about to settle down to the normal sort of life that we all lead. Up until now it had been one of adventure and excitement around the world, from the U-Boat stalking grounds of the cold North Atlantic to the Normandy Landings, and later Sumatra. Then years under the hot African sun in Kenya, but now he was back to good old Blighty. His roller coaster ride of luck, chance and fate was about to slow down to the regular beat of British life.

England was not the dark rubble filled country in recession that he had left all those years earlier. Although Norman had popped back from time to time on holiday, when he arrived back for good the swinging sixties were here.

The launch of the Telstar Satellite had brought American television across the Atlantic. Cliff Richards was singing his heart out and a new band from Liverpool was sending the girls wild with *"She loves you yeah, yeah, yeah"*. The Pill was available as a contraceptive for the first time, and Carnaby Street in London was dressing people in bright brave fashions. Britain was alive with miniskirts and free love.

Norman and Doris decided to settle down in the coastal town of Eastbourne to bring up their two sons. Eastbourne was the ideal spot on the coast near the sea that he had come to love so dearly, a place he had passed countless times on his war convoys.

He popped up to see his dad who had retired from St Neots to Luton and had become an expert bowls player. He also went up there to pick up his belongings that his dad had stored for him.

He was shocked to find out that Ernest had given his Hetchins away! Norman had a sneaky feeling that Ernest had sold it to pay for a season ticket to the local football club! "You've done what?"

"Well it just sat there for years going rusty."He mumbled to Norman as a feeble excuse and hurried off to the garden.

Norman was disappointed but when he opened the garage door he was delighted to find that his dad had given his later Hetchins bicycle away, not his beloved early 1935 model with the curly stays. Norman had got his later Hetchins with gratuity money anyway, so really it had not cost him a penny.

When it came time for Norman to leave he made sure, even though it was awkward, to take his remaining bike with him when he left! He also took his Japanese officer's sword and luger, just in case Ernest was short for a season ticket at his favorite Luton FC the following year!

Norman and Doris settle down to life in Eastbourne.

Amongst the many things Norman had left behind in Kenya was the large furniture-size wireless. He decided to replace it with one of the new-fangled transistor radios. Amazed at the small size, he bought some batteries and rushed home to play with his new mini-marvel. He put in the batteries and turned on his Sony transistor radio. He was then stunned into silence when the first shocking words came out.

"We regret to inform you that that today at 12:30 Central Standard Time the President of America, John Fitzgerald Kennedy, known to many as JFK was assassinated. He was shot at least three times and pronounced dead by doctors at 1:00 pm at Parkland Memorial Hospital in Dallas, Texas. He was 46. Lee Harvey Oswald, an employee of the Texas School Book Depository, has been arrested and charged with his assassination."

Norman turned the radio off and sat in stunned disbelief. Doris came into the room drying a cup with a tea towel. "Well dear how's the new radio?"

"Bloody awful," Norman replied shaking his head at a rather surprised Doris. "Just bloody awful."

Later Norman decided his life in Eastbourne really didn't need a gun, so he donated his German luger to the Redoubt Fortress Military Museum on the seafront, where it remained until it disappeared in the 1990's.

However his samurai sword was kept behind the wardrobe just in case some burglar thought he would have a go. What a surprise the intruder would have had coming up against the old Kimbolton School boxing champion, all five-foot of him, wielding a samurai sword and screaming in Swahili!

Life moved on and Norman, Doris and the kids settled in to their new home. Norman started teaching at the new secondary modern school, Ratton, in the beginning of 1964.

Norman would cycle to Ratton each day, and at the end of a day's teaching bring back the pupils books for marking on his bike-rack. Norman taught Religious Education at Ratton and used his experiences from his many remarkable acquaintances over the years as examples for his pupils. From Leslie Weatherhead who had preached so fiercely at the City Temple in London in 1936 to Archbishop L J Beecher who had attended Jeremy's christening in African. He installed in the young bright-eyed lads at Ratton an interest in religious studies, regardless of whether they believed in God or not.

January 1965 started with the sad news that the great Winston Churchill had finally passed away at his Hyde Park home. Winston had been ill for some time and loathed being an old man. All his later public appearances, where he was wheeled out to the crowds, show the face of a broken man. He had once been the toast of the world, but in later years, in failing health, he hated every second of his own mortality.

Winston had thought himself immortal, he braved every dangerous mission, every hare-brained experience in the certain knowledge that he would never die. He would walk through the Blitz with bombs raining down and know he would not get hurt. In later years it was a terrible realisation to him that he too would have to face death.

Crowds had gathered outside his home waiting anxiously for news of the 90 year old statesman. His wife, Clementine, held his hand as he slipped into a deep sleep from which he never woke.

The leader of the British, the bulldog that would never surrender, the flawed but brilliant man had finally left this mortal coil. The country now had to stand on its own feet for the first time, and Britain could never be the same again.

Hundreds of thousands of mourners passed quietly by his coffin in Westminster Hall where he laid in state, the first politician since Gladstone to have that honour bestowed upon him.

When he was moved out of the hall to St Paul's the only sound was the horse's hoofs on the cobbles and the sobbing from the crowds as his body passed by on a gun carriage. The crowds were hushed as Big Ben struck its mournful tones. Winston's body made slow progress through the streets of London towards St Paul's Cathedral. His funeral was the most watched television event in the history of television to that date. Dozens of cameras along his route beamed pictures to a watching somber world.

At St Paul's, Lady Clementine and Winston's children led the procession. Inside, the cathedral was packed with representatives from all four corners of the earth. The Queen and many other members of the Royal Family looked on as his coffin moved along the central aisle. Prime Minister, Harold Wilson, bowed his head in honour as the coffin moved by.

After the service Winston was piped aboard the launch, MV-*Havengore*, for a voyage up Old Father Thames.

Churchill's body being moved aboard MV *Havengore*.

As his body went along the river from Tower Pier to Festival Pier dockers who had fought for King and Country, like *'Basher'* Harris and *'Dockyard'* Pete, lowered their cranes in salute.

A 19 gun salute by the Royal Artillery announced the start of another journey and an RAF fly-past roared overhead with 16 Lightning Fighters. They brought welcome noise to the eerie silence that cut the day. Later, from Waterloo Station, he was placed on the Battle of Britain train called, *the Winston Churchill,* and taken to Handborough.

All along his final journey men, women and children stood as close to the tracks as they could to pay their last respects, farmers removed their caps in their fields as the specially painted train made its way slowly to its destination. And then finally, as per his wishes, he was laid to rest at the family plot at St Martin's Church at Bladon in Oxfordshire.

Sir Winston Leonard Spencer-Churchill, Knight of the Garter, was buried less than a mile from Blenheim Palace where he had been born in 1874.

Chapter 31
World Cup Fever

The pages of life turned again, and 1966 was a much happier year. Football fever was here and Norman, always the keen footballer, was dribbling a football around his kids in the garden when they were not glued to his super new television set.

Jeremy and Christopher

Initially England was not seen as a team of much hope, bookies gave them odds of 9-1 and they say that even the London gangsters the Kray twins in the East End were placing bets. As Alf Ramsey sent his lads out in their friendly against Poland, no one was holding their breath. A boring 1-1 draw gave the papers ammunition to slag off the players and the manager.

After warm up matches, teams from all over the globe started to descend on London. The twice World Cup champions arrived from Brazil with heroes such as Pele that kids had only seen on cigarette cards. The Portuguese team came with Eusebio de Silva Ferreira a ferocious attacker, who was so popular that he was later immortalised in wax at Madame Tussauds.

Queen Elizabeth, with Phillip by her side, opened the 8th World Football Championships at Wembley. The first England match was against Uruguay on 11 July. A nervous England team struggled to hold Uruguay to a 0-0 draw. Alf Ramsey made feeble excuses and the papers cut him to shreds.

Next round, England v Mexico. Bobby Charlton whacked home a beauty and later in the 75th minute Roger Hunt, the Liverpool player, scored again. The crowd was in an uproar. By now the people of England started to dream of an England final on the hallowed Wembley turf. But up next were the dreaded French team with players like the formidable midfielder Joseph Bonnel.

England's defence was superb and on the 20 July, after the French goal keeper had to be replaced at the last moment, the two teams ran out on to the pitch. Hunt was again in action and after a pass by Bobby Charlton he scored his first then at the 76th minute Callaghan dropped it to him again and he put it in the back of the French net. England was victorious 2-0. Soon every shop and home in the country seemed to be flying English flags. The press had gone from slaughtering the players to calling them heroes. Their manager Alf Ramsey could suddenly walk on water.

The impossible now seemed possible, England was in the semi-final but they were against one of the greatest teams in the world, Portugal. The Portuguese team was a power house of talent, and Norman held his breath as he watched on his television.

The television set needed warming up and several tweaks on the rear dial before the picture would stop rolling up and down. Norman would put the TV on half an hour before the match to get the set just right. Of course there was also the proverbial slap on the side of the box when the picture disappeared altogether!

The game was hectic, the crowd sighed and cheered, screamed and hid their faces each time the Portuguese attack got near, but in the 30th minute Bobby Charlton once again ploughed a beauty into the opposition's net. England went hysterical and in the 79th minute Hurst played the ball to Charlton and he dispatched it once more into the back of the Portuguese net. England were on a roll but a penalty by Eusebio gave Portugal a chance. England played like gladiators attacking every ball, every player, and when the final whistle blew the score was England 2 Portugal 1. Eusebio broke down and cried as his team left the stadium.

No one could believe it, England, against all the odds, would be in the World Cup Final at Wembley. In the streets men chanted, cheered and waved flags, football clackers were swiveled around and around until the kids wrists hurt.

World Cup Willy mascots were shoved in windows and workplaces. England was ablaze with England hats, whistles and scarves. Every sentence uttered by every person in England that July of 1966 had the word football in it.

World Cup Willie 1966

On 30 July, 1966, 22 players stepped out into the Wembley sunshine to a crowd of over 97, 000. The place was packed to the rafters, and outside the ground thousands had turned up just to be at Wembley, listening to the match on car radios and portable wirelesses. The Royal Marine Band played, but few could hear it above the chanting and shouting. They say over a thousand supporters lost their voices that day at Wembley. They also say that the 1966 England football team was arguably the greatest England team that has ever played. They had shrugged off all the early moans and groans, ignored the papers and did what every great Englishman does in their hour of need, they put their best foot forward and gave it their all.

England was playing against the mighty West German team who had slaughtered all on-comers to get to the final. They were not going to be beaten by England again. Their German pride was at stake. Alf Ramsey apparently said to his lads as they went out onto the pitch, "You've beaten them once, now do it again."

The match was an epic struggle. Germany started the scoring as Helmut Haller popped one past Gordon Banks. A few minutes later Bobby Moore shot up the field, passed to Geoff Hurst who equaled the score, 1-1. The roar coming from the stadium could be heard miles away.

The game laboured on in a nervous state, until late in the match Martin Peters made it 2-1 to England. Now Germany had nothing to lose, they played like men possessed and in the 90th minute, as the referees whistle was in his mouth to blow for the end, Wolfgang Weber made it 2-2.

The match had to go to extra time. English fans could not believe that they had been cheated from victory right at the last second.

Extra time was fraught, but Alan Ball made a superb pass to Geoff Hurst, who blasted a shot at goal. It bounced off the bar down to the pitch, and no one knew if it was in or not. The noise from the crowd disappeared to a hush as the referee took his time and went to consult with the linesman. As the crowd waited, the referee blew his whistle—goal.

The noise nearly lifted Wembley off the ground as the England fans simultaneously cheered. England was ahead 3-2. Low scoring finals were the norm, as the two opposing teams were usually unbeatable, but to have a score of 3-2, surely the Germans could not come back?

But come back they did. As the minutes ticked, they seemed like hours. The Germans kept up tremendous pressure on the England defence, pushing, probing, attacking down one flank, then the next. As the seconds counted down to the final whistle, spectators could no longer hold their breath. Some even climbed the short barriers and started coming on the pitch.

The commentator Ken Wolstenholme, was also shouting with his hoarse voice, *"Some people are on the pitch…They think it's all over,"* he carried on breathlessly as Bobby Moore made a perfect pass in front of Geoff Hurst. Geoff, at full speed blasted the ball into the back of the German net. Ken, in the same breathless sentence, roared, *"IT IS NOW."*

The final whistle blew seconds later and England's greatest football match had finished, beating Germany 4-2. Geoff Hurst had been the first and only man to score a hat-trick in a World Cup Final.

The German team wept, the England team wept. England seemed to rise out of the sea as millions leapt into the air. Tough miners in Yorkshire hugged their sons for the first time, and hardened men knelt and shed tears of joy. A nation had the greatest instantaneous uplifting in their history as for the first time, because of technology, every person simultaneously heard and saw the result on that glorious summer day of July 30, 1966.

The solid gold cup was ready. It had been stolen earlier in the year but Pickles the dog had found it under a bush wrapped in an old newspaper. His owner received the enormous reward of £5,000. That was one lucky walk!

Queen Elizabeth held out the golden chalice to Bobby Moore, who was too choked to talk properly. Every man woman and boy who lived through that day in England remembered it. The patriotic fever lasted for months, and they say that even the products made in the factories of England over the next few months seemed to last longer, as they were made by people who were happy, a whole nation was happy.

Chapter 32
Time to slow down

As the country got back to its normal pace Norman cycled down to Ratton School each day.

Norman and Doris in retirement.

One day melted in to another and the months then years flowed by. Finally, after a few more administration tasks as Assistant Education Officer for several colleges, Norman retired.

To celebrate his retirement Norman, at 65, took his boys on an 88 mile trek along the South Downs Way, stopping at bed & breakfasts and inns along the way.

Norman slowed down a little in later life, and indulged in his love of golf, getting his handicap down at the Willingdon Golf Club and later becoming an honorary member for life.

Norman would help the Samaritans, and for nearly 20 years listened patiently to people's problems.

Occasionally his old tropical disease would bubble up on his forehead and he would have it removed at the local hospital. "Probably kept me alive, that thing I picked up 70 years ago," Norman would laugh. He settled into retirement and let the years poodle past.

Willingdon Golf club veterans with club pro and tiny Norman on the right.

2010

When Doris died from cancer, like his beloved mother many years before he collected her ashes and scattered them in her favourite bluebell woods at Chiddingly and on her beloved South Downs.

Each day the Daily Telegraph crossword was attacked with vigour and the world news thoroughly investigated. Ninety-one years of Norman's life had gone by, and he would slowly walk up to the post box most days to post letters that he had written to former friends and colleagues. "I don't like to move faster than one knot nowadays just in case I take a tumble." Norman once told me with a little smile, as we meandered along together chatting.

Over endless cups of tea in his rambling old house, we would talk about days gone by. We chatted about the moon landings or the Channel Tunnel, which Norman decided would have come in handy during the Normandy invasion. The latest inventions would leave him baffled. I wouldn't even know how to turn on a computer, he would tell me. "I used to have trouble connecting the accumulator to the wireless in 1928 and that only had two wires!"

At Christmas Norman would fetch out a tin of his favourite Scottish Highland shortbread and we would celebrate with a little sherry—or two. During the winter the huge old boiler would rattle and bang like someone trying to get into the house. "Old ghosts Alex, just old ghosts," Norman would say to me and smile.

Norman at 91 with his samurai sword from 1945.

Norman has lived all alone in these later years and the large house is full of dusty memories. When he talked about the war or his life, he would often say that he hardly mentioned his achievements as he had met, and seen, so many remarkable people during his long life that had achieved so much more than him. In his empty house it was hard to imagine a time when Norman and Doris lived there with their children, and for a time Ernest was with them and Doris's Sister, Ivy, with her husband too. Every bedroom was full and meal times were cooked in turn by Doris and Ivy, and served up to a noisy table. Now the house was as quiet as a church mouse, with just the wind and the boiler to keep Norman company.

Norman could remember times from 85 years ago as if they had happened yesterday. Often the best memories are the ones set in stone, and for Norman these were his early days. His eyes would sparkle when he talked about his time at St Neots Elementary, or watching the new magnesium strip on his dad's flash sizzle when he took pictures in his studio.

"You see Alex most things seem to go in cycles. Look at the annihilation of the Jews. At the same time as I was fighting the Germans they were also systematically trying to remove a race of people from this world.

When the camps came to light just as the war was coming to an end, I looked on in disbelief at the men, women and children, riddled with illnesses and covered in lice, living the most wretched existence possible. Our hearts just could not behold such suffering. The next thing you know the Jewish people had carved out the new nation of Israel, so that their children could grow up in a world where the genocide of their race could never be allowed. The Berlin Wall went up and the Berlin Wall came down again. I remember seeing it go up and I remember seeing it being chipped away bit by bit, stone by stone one November in 1989."

"I saw Disco fever spark up in the 1970's. I hope I won't be around to see it come back! I never could dance like Travolta! I don't think anyone could. He made dancing look—somehow masculine, where as I, well, say no more. Coming on as the Christmas Fairy at Kakamega probably scarred me for life.

When you have lived as long as I have, you get the time to see how this world works. There are few surprises left for me now."

Norman had worked out a near perfect system to survive on his own as the years rolled by. A gardener came, a cleaner also called, shopping was delivered by Christine—his daughter-in-law. His son, Chris, kept a constant eye on him to make sure everything was okay while Jeremy was abroad and his niece, Jane, regularly popped in sorting out any problems. Old friends like Geoff dropped by and chatted about old days. Even a retired bishop would stop by to try, in vain, to get Norman to turn back to the church.

Each night he would pour out his glass of whisky, add a drop of water and toast the world, *"Up spirits and stand fast for the Holy Ghost."*

Day-by-day in his happy-go-lucky way Norman had grown old.

The balance in life that Norman found seemed to me that he had discovered the secret of being comfortable with himself. He is at peace in his quiet slow world, as if he had spent years studying mediation and discovered an elusive calm that avoids the rest of us. He has no fear of death; to him it is part of life and to be expected, almost welcomed. At 91 he has lived longer than most, and could have been wiped out many times in his hectic journey through life. He thinks of himself as privileged to have seen so much and lived through such an amazing century, witnessing first-hand the dawn of our modern age.

"Norman have you ever heard of a Hetchins bicycle?" I idly asked as we walked back down Church Street one sunny afternoon. I had been out for a walk with Rolly, my faithful old dog, and met Norman at the post box. Rolly dragged behind us almost as slowly as Norman. They were perfectly matched for speed, both winding home, not a care in the world.

"Ah, Hetchins, unusual name Alex, why do you ask?"

"Well when I was a kid we had a curly-stay Hetchins, amazing machine. It was stolen and I thought you might have heard of them, as they were in their prime in your era?"

"When we get home you come round to my shed and I'll show you something."

"That's an offer Norman!" We both laughed and carried on the last few yards to Norman's house. Round the back of his old house was a large rambling garden that Doris had once kept immaculate, but since her death Norman had just kept up the basics.

Norman got to his old shed and pulled open the creaky door. He went in and shuffled around for a while. "Come have a look at this Alex." I moved in closer, and as my eyes became accustomed to the light, I made out the shape of an old rusty bike lying under some junk. "Pull it out Alex."

After a bit of heaving and shoving, brushing away cobwebs and some tins crashing off a shelf, the old lump came out. The tyres were almost flat and most of it was covered in rust, but there was an unmistakable gleam to it and a well oiled chain. I rubbed the main tube and slowly, like a ghost ship rising from the depths, the words cleared on the frame, Hetchins.

"Didn't expect that did you Alex?

"No way Norman, where on earth…?"

"Take her she's yours. I see my son Jerry is riding your old bike anyway, so we'll call it a swap. I had her reconditioned by Horace Heath down in Cavendish Place during the 1970's, but since I gave up cycling she has been in the shed. I know you'll fix her up a treat and I won't be going anywhere on it."

"Norman I don't know what to say, how long have you had her? Where did you get her from? How old is she? It's a miracle."

"Not quite a miracle, but certainly lucky." Norman laughed. "Now slow down Alex, It's a long story and starts way back before the 1936 Olympics. I'll put the kettle on and over a cup of tea I'll tell you all about it."

The End

Norman aged 10.

Norman at 91.

About the Author

About the author "Born of a Russian/French father and Austrian/English mother, I grew up in 1960's England and witnessed the birth of our modern age. One of six boys our house was always an explosion of noise. From this early experience I now cherish my quiet moments. My friends call me an introvert. Originally I went through the state schooling system but things changed dramatically. My parents were in the manufacturing of baby goods and after the Miners Strikes of the 1970's caused the power across the country to be turned off early each night a massive baby-boom soon followed. The business flourished and I was suddenly bundled off to private school. One second I was almost invisible playing conkers in a class of 44 the next at boarding school learning Latin with 11 classmates. Quite a shock! My old headmaster at Ratton did not find out for a month that I had been moved! Later I studied engineering and eventually became a self-employed engineer and after many years a master craftsman running my own specialised business in sewing machinery, a trade that I have known since a child. I still live in my hometown of Eastbourne with my wife and kids. I carry on the trade that I grew up with around the rural Southeast corner of England collecting fascinating stories along the way."

Inspiring stories from fascinating people

By

Alex I Askaroff

WILLINGDON PARK DRIVE
EASTBOURNE BN22 0DG
UNITED KINGDOM

PATCHES OF HEAVEN ISBN 0-9539410-4-3
SKYLARK COUNTRY ISBN 0-9539410-2-7
HIGH STREETS & HEDGEROWS ISBN 0-9539410-3-5
TALES FROM THE COAST ISBN 978-0-9539410-5-6
CORNER OF THE KINGDOM ISBN 978-1-61179-067-2
SUSSEX BORN AND BRED ISBN: 978-1-935585-22-0

Sussex Born and Bred

ISBN: 978-1-935585-22-0

Not so long ago, doctors made house calls and fresh milk was delivered daily to our doors. Such consideration has gone from the modern world forever - or has it? Alex Askaroff, a Sussex lad, left a thriving family business in specialty textiles to become a travelling sewing machine repairman, carrying on a disappearing trade that he has known since a child.

This master craftsman also has the enthusiasm of a poet and a pure love of story-telling. As Alex brings sewing machines back to life he also picks up local stories, history and gossip. And what stories they are! From the lady who was presented, by Alex, with a long lost family heirloom hidden in her sewing machine for 60 years to an encounter with the ghost of Arthur Conan Doyle. Vic the old gardener who practices the old ways of determining when to plant his crops with his bum! Cross-dressing "Peacehaven Pansies" and their flamboyant friends are here as well. From kings to conkers this book touches on the, often eccentric, people who make up Sussex.

Alex has spent over 20 years slowly collecting priceless anecdotes of the lives, hilarity, wisdom and history of his Corner of the Kingdom.

Corner of the Kingdom

ISBN: 978-1-61179-067-2

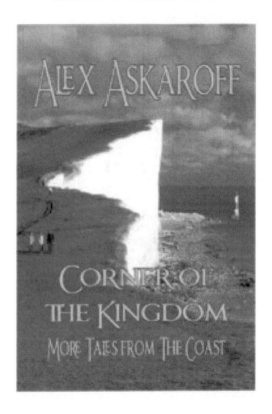

Sussex Born and Bred was launched in 40 countries worldwide and was one of the first books on the Apple iPad.

Sussex Born and Bred is a series of short true stories in which Alex Askaroff brings both England's history and her people vividly to life. The stories were collected around Sussex from local people, and their deep insight into our beautiful corner of the world, old tales of ghosts and folklore is mesmerising. Although they are local stories the book has had world-wide appeal with Alex's easy writing style and humour. Sussex Born and Bred contains stories like the ghost of Vivien Leigh in Blackboys, Eastbourne tailors who worked for Queen Elizabeth, cockney royalty, war veterans, hop-pickers who picked while the Battle of Britain exploded above them, everyone from Salvador Dali to Picasso and William Duke of Normandy. It is an unforgettable portrait of Sussex and its inhabitants.

In *Norman, A Journey Through Time,* Alex Askaroff relates one man's life and career against the turmoil of World War Two. It is a glorious tale, although not without sadness, and clearly demonstrates how even global conflict need not dissuade a determined spirit. Norman is revealed as a strong, but sensitive character, one who proved more than able to meet the demands his country made on him, and particularly adept at turning stumbling blocks into stepping stones.

This is a gentle, but informative book that will find a home amongst those who remember an era that is all but lost, and may well open the eyes of those who came later.

Askaroff's timely reflections on the period and events certainly give an excellent perspective to the story.

Alaric Bond

Author

Fighting Sail Series

Printed in Great Britain
by Amazon